The Encyclopedia of Ornament

HENRY SHAW

DOVER PUBLICATIONS, INC.
Mineola, New York

Bibliographical Note

This Dover edition, first published by Dover Publications, Inc., in 2016, is a republication of the work originally published by William Pickering, London, in 1842. The original color images have been relocated to the inside covers for this edition.

International Standard Book Number

ISBN-13: 978-0-486-80740-9
ISBN-10: 0-486-80740-1

Manufactured in the United States by LSC Communications
80740102 2017
www.doverpublications.com

PREFACE.

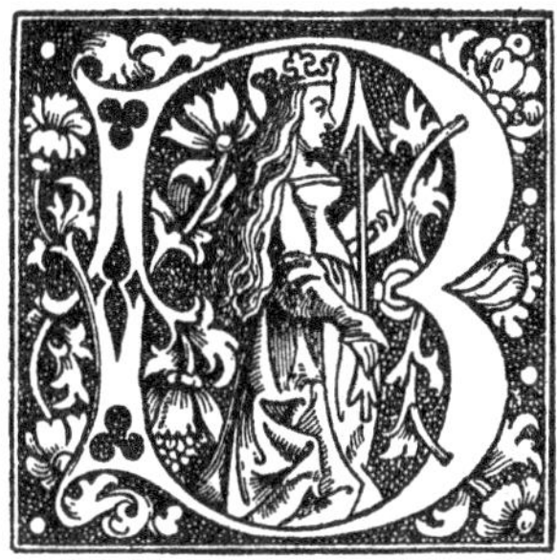

EFORE the appearance of the present work, the object of which is to give a selection of the purest and best specimens of ornament of all kinds and of all ages, many books on the subject of ornament had been given to the public; but, in general, they were either specially restricted to one class or one style, or imperfect as giving faulty or inaccurate examples, or difficult of access to most of those who require them for practical purposes, on account of the expensive form in which they were published. The Author has endeavoured, as far as possible in a work of moderate expense, to remove these difficulties. It has been his study to give faithful representations of authentic models belonging to each particular class of designs, of affording a direct reference to some of the best examples of the several styles and periods, and therefore furnishing hints for a selection of parts which when combined may produce a new arrangement of equal elegance; thus constituting a mass of materials from which the artist or manufacturer may derive a succession of entirely novel designs. Each style has its peculiar character, and this must pervade all fresh combinations to make them pleasing and satisfactory. The ornament of different nations has its distinctive features, and these so vary as to illustrate particular epochs. A knowledge of these necessary points can only be attained by an opportunity of studying from the originals themselves, or from copies drawn with strict adherence to their peculiar characteristics. On this point the Author trusts that the present Collection will be highly conducive to the enlargement of correct taste in all branches of decorative art.

Greece and Rome have left us specimens of foliage in which natural objects have been copied with classical elegance; but in the Middle Ages and Oriental examples we find a profusion of ornamental detail, rich in invention, of a grotesque and fanciful nature. At the period of the Renaissance, the elegant taste of the ancients was blended with mediæval richness and Eastern fancy. We look for the best specimens of painted glass in windows from the twelfth century to the fifteenth; for florid ornamental architecture in buildings of the same period; for carvings and engraved ornaments, bindings of books, jewellery, embroidery, ornamental plate, and furniture, in the sixteenth century. We have elegant and rich designs of drapery during the Middle Ages. Foliage and scroll-work are peculiarly bold and effective in the twelfth and thirteenth centuries; and throughout the fourteenth, fifteenth, and sixteenth centuries, arabesques are abundant.

The present Volume contains Examples of most of these Classes, taken from the period at which each was in its greatest perfection, and the specimens are arranged in chronological order. Architectural Ornaments are given from works of various dates; stained glass from York, Durham, Canterbury, Salisbury, Cologne, Chartres, &c.; painted tiles of the thirteenth and fifteenth centuries, from Westminster, and Great Malvern in Worcestershire; carvings in wood and panels of the fifteenth and sixteenth centuries; rich ironwork of the thirteenth century, from the doors of the church of Nôtre Dame at Paris; ornamental drapery, velvet hangings, &c., from designs of the fifteenth century; lace and needlework of the seventeenth; bindings of books of the sixteenth century; and designs for jewellery, plate, and other ornamental articles, by Hans Holbein and contemporary artists.

To the practical designer, therefore, this work is offered as a useful collection of pure studies of ancient works of art; while the amateur will find in it a correct series of illustration of the progress of ornamental design during a long period of history.

LIST OF PLATES

TO THE ENCYCLOPÆDIA OF ORNAMENT.

LIST OF PLATES TO THE ENCYCLOPÆDIA OF ORNAMENT.

25. Ornament from the soffit of an arch in the Gallilee of Durham Cathedral.
26. Ornaments in stone from Southwell Church and Furness Abbey.
27. Ornamental Tracery from the Abbey of Jumieges in Normandy.
28. Ornaments on the Box containing the Seal of the Royal Hospital of St. Catherine, Regent's Park.
29. Ornaments on an ancient Chair in St. Mary's Hall, Coventry.
30. Ornaments carved in wood at Hildesheim and Salzwedel.
31. Ornamental Carvings in Wood.
32. Ornaments from the Palace of Heidelberg.
33. Coloured Ornaments from the monuments of Sophia and Maria, daughters of James I and from that of the Countess of Oxford and family in Westminster Abbey. These ornaments are carved in low flat relief in alabaster, the raised parts being gilt and the spaces between filled in black.
34. Ornaments of the beginning of the 17th century, containing a panel with a shield and coronet, and two inlaid ornaments.
35. Heraldic Panels, in the possession of Thos. Willement, F.S.A.
36. Panels in Marble, from the Façade of the Certosa di Pavia.
37. From a Picture by an early German painter of the date of 1472.
38. From a painted oak Screen in Worstead Church, Norfolk. This screen is one of the most interesting examples of painted architecture in England.
39. Pendants from St. Stephen's Chapel, Westminster.
40. Three Sides of a Pilaster in the cloister of St. Sauveur at Aix, in Provence.
41. Designs for Plate, from a very valuable collection of drawings by Van Swol, in the print room of the British Museum.
42. Border of Stained Glass in the Royal Abbey of St. Denys, near Parys.
43. Stained Glass in the possession of Thomas Willement, F.S.A.

44–45. Stained Glass from Canterbury Cathedral.

46. Stained Glass from Salisbury Cathedral.
47. Stained Glass from the Chapter House of York Cathedral.
48. Stained Glass from Southwell Church, Nottinghamshire.
49. Stained Glass from the church of Altenberg, near Cologne.
50. Stained Glass from the Sacristy of the Cathedral at Chartres.
51. Stained Glass from the entrance to the Sacristy of the Cathedral at Chartres.
52. From Stained Glass, and from Needle work. The stained glass from the beautiful window recently erected in St. George's Church, Hanover Square, and formerly in the Cathedral at Mechlin.
53. A Staircase, from a drawing in the possession of C. J. Richardson, Esq. F.S.A.
54. A Design for Tapestry, from a drawing in the possession of C. J. Richardson, Esq. F.S.A.

Inside Covers: Painted Tiles from the Chapter House, Westminster. From drawings by L. N. Cottingham, Esq. F.S.A., at whose suggestion this beautiful floor was uncovered Jan. 1st, 1831. One quarter only of each figure is given to allow room for four varieties.

Painted Tiles from Great Malvern Church, Worcestershire.

The Encyclopedia of Ornament

Date about 1500.

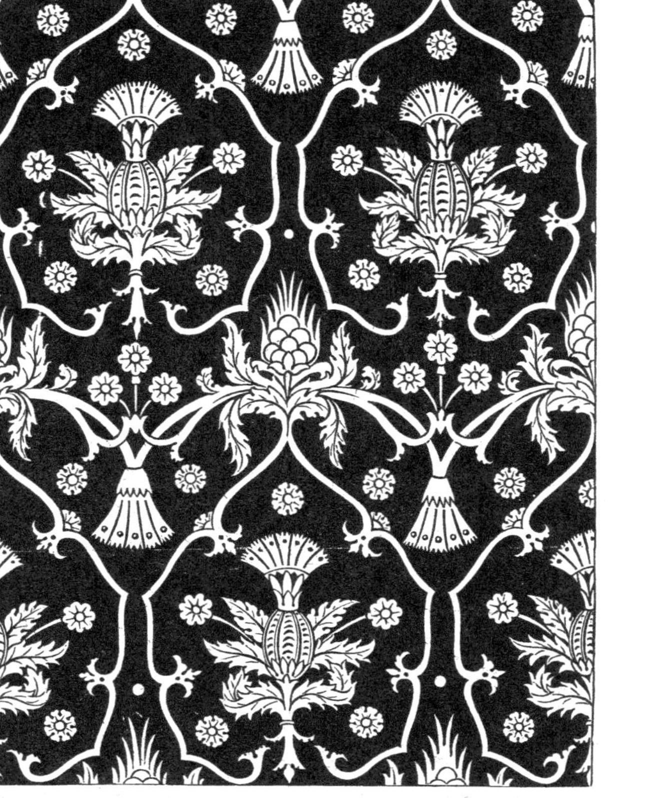

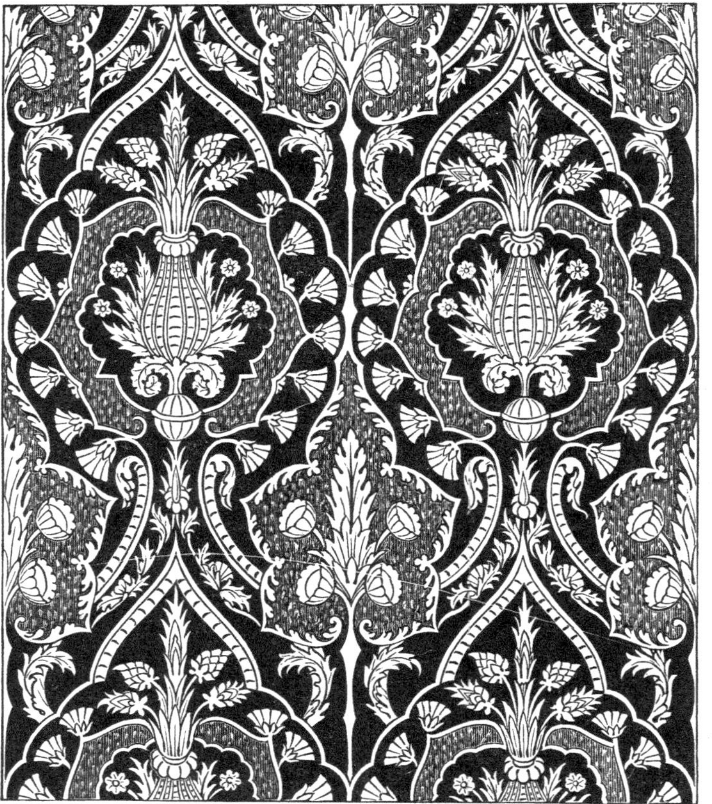

ANTE-PENDIUMS.

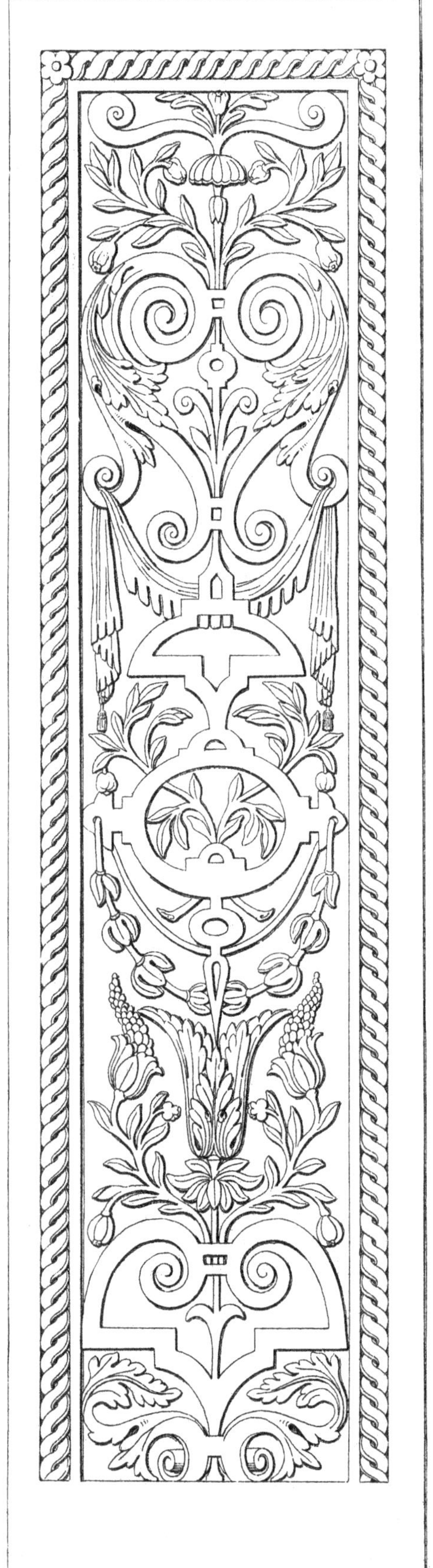

Arabesque on the lining of a Door,

Palace of Heidelberg.

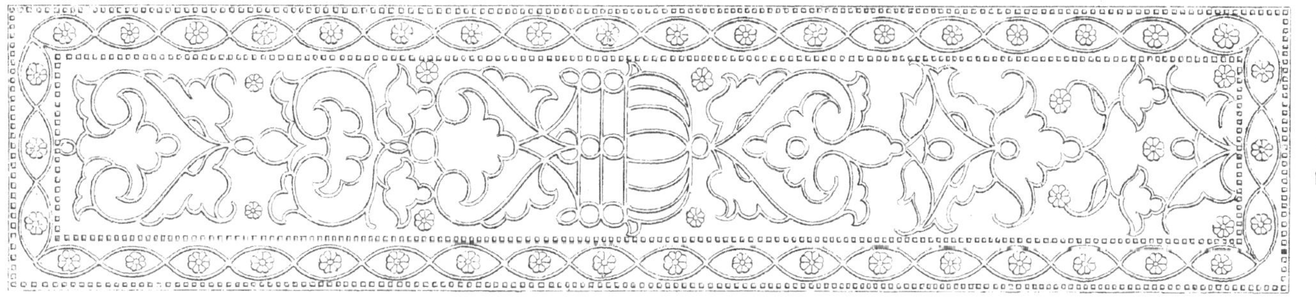

Front.

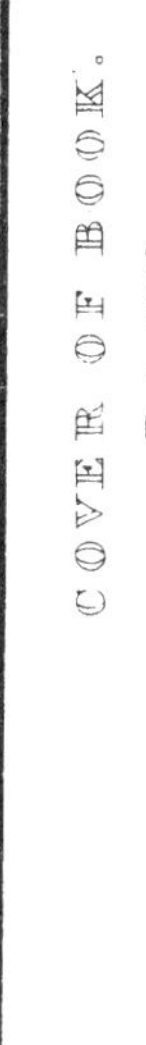

COVER OF BOOK.

Date 1548

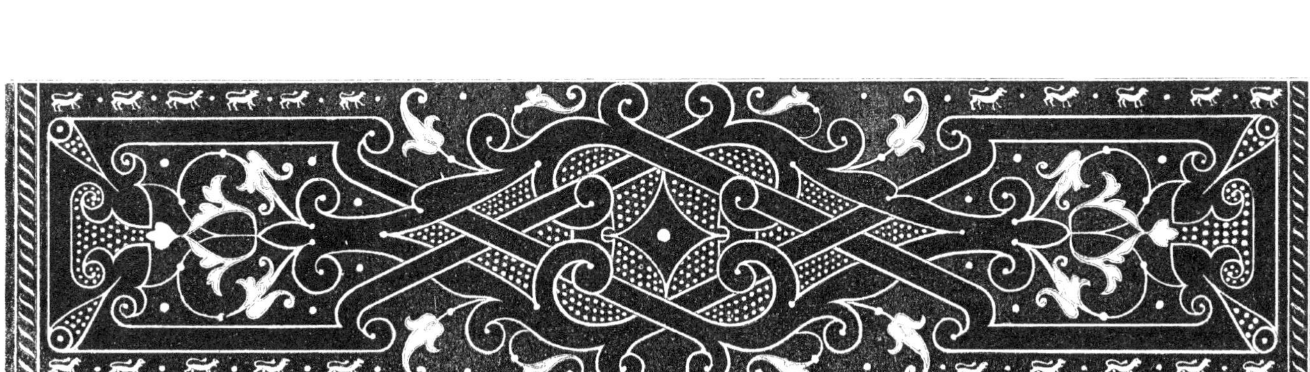

Back.

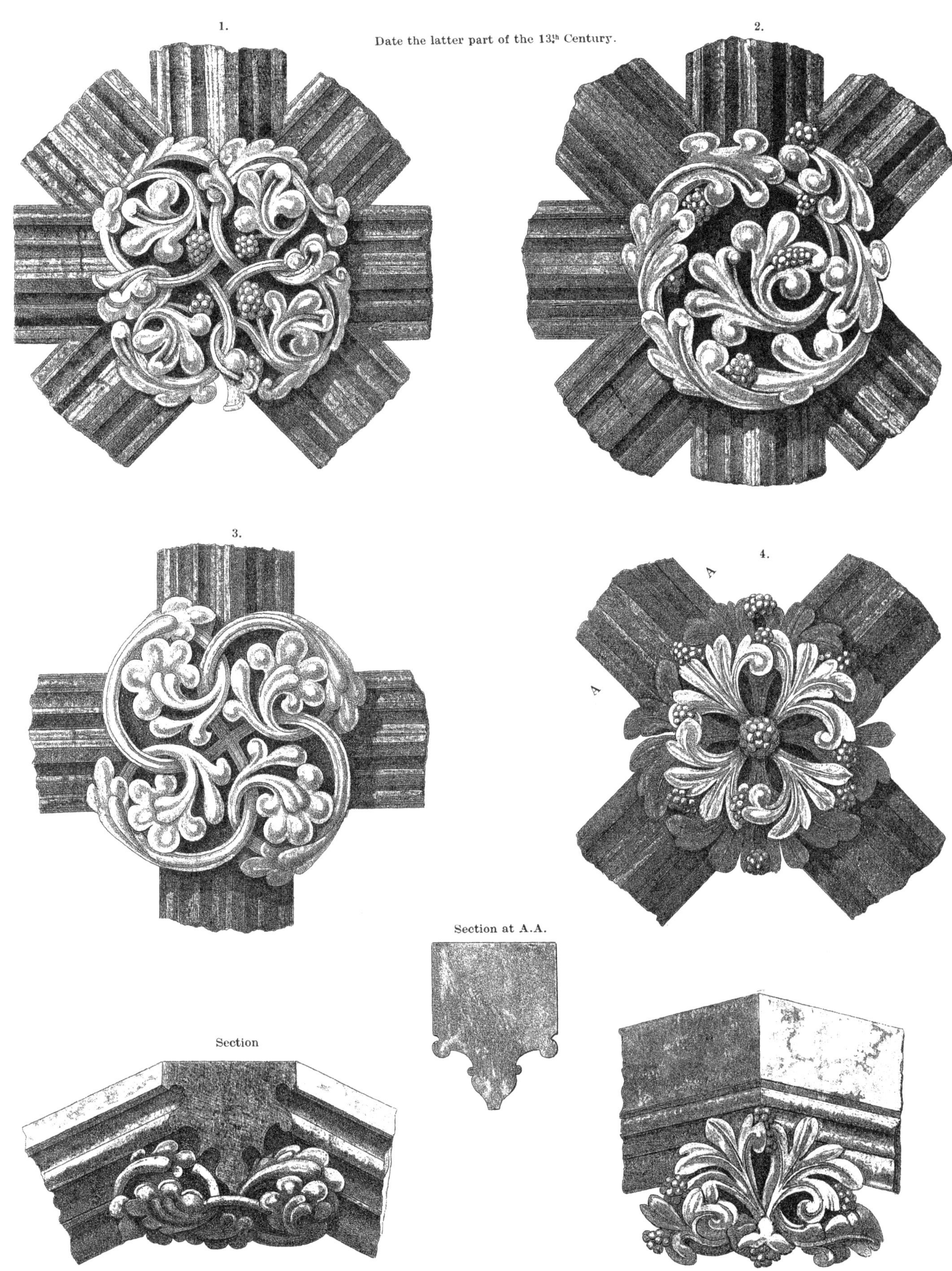

Nos 1, 2, 3. From Southwell Church, Nottinghamshire.
No 4. From the passage leading out of the Cloisters,
into the Chapter House, Westminster Abbey.

Drawn & Engraved by Henry Shaw.

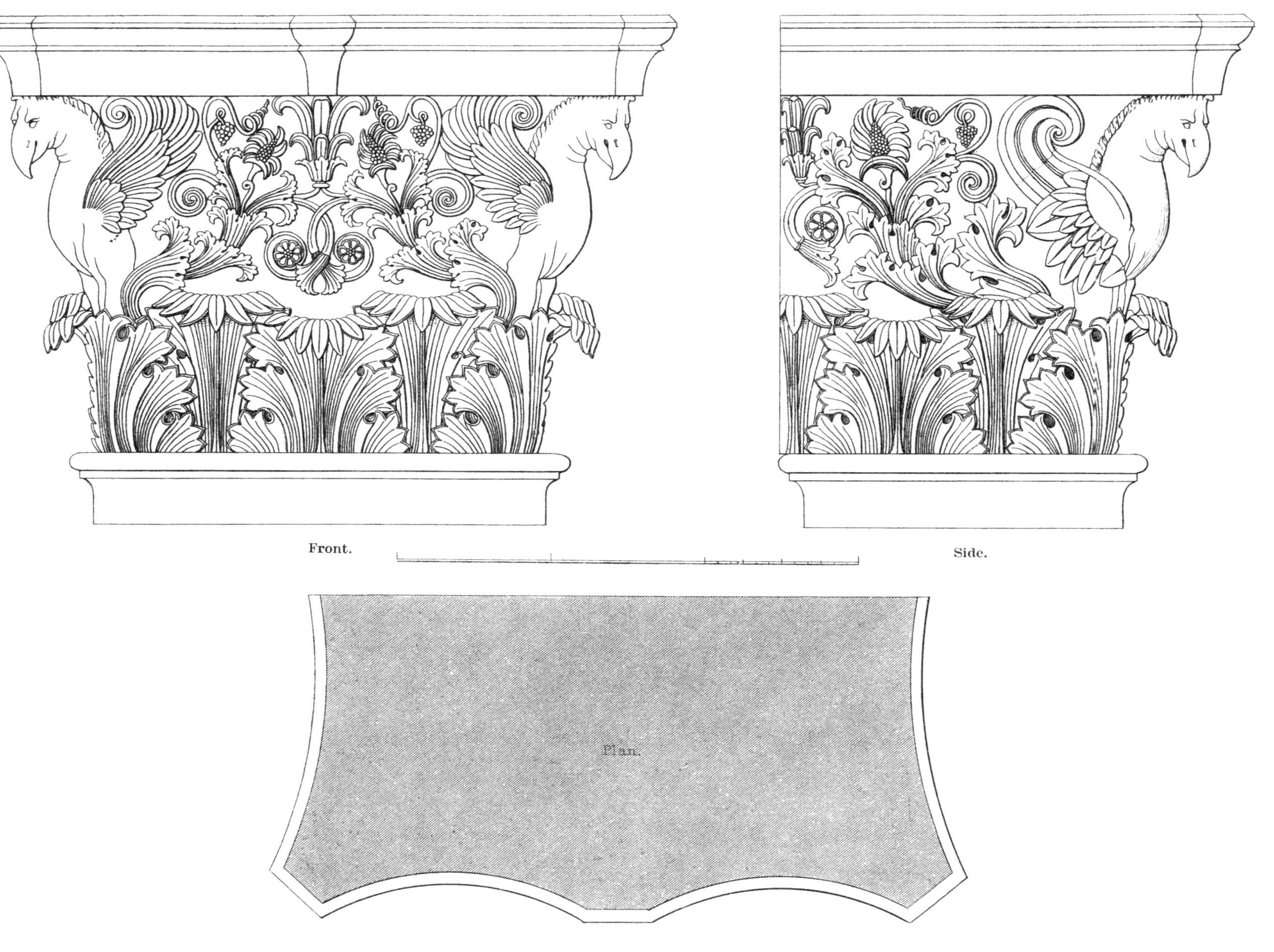

CAPITAL OF PILASTERS IN THE TEMPLE OF ELEUSIS, AT ATHENS.

Drawn & Eng^d by H. Shaw.

Date the latter part of the 13th Century.

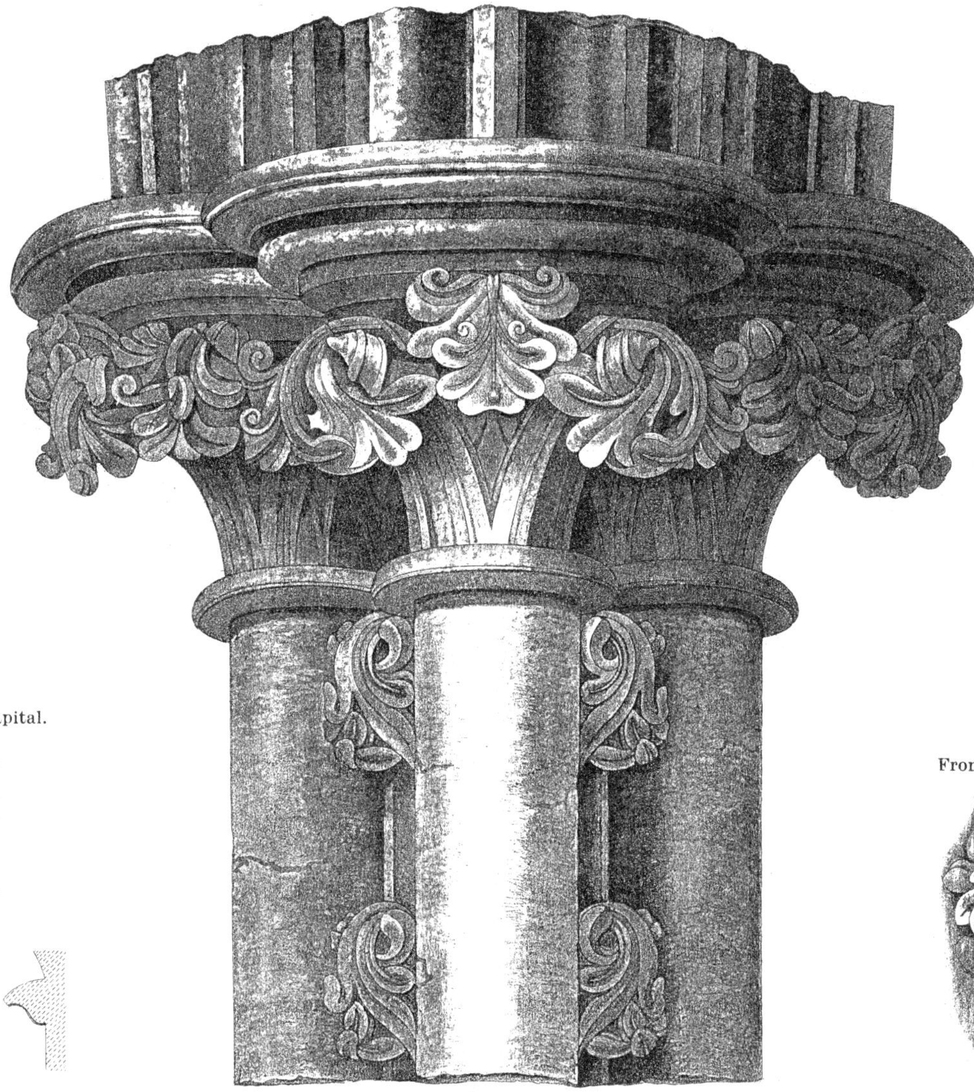

Mouldings of the Capital.

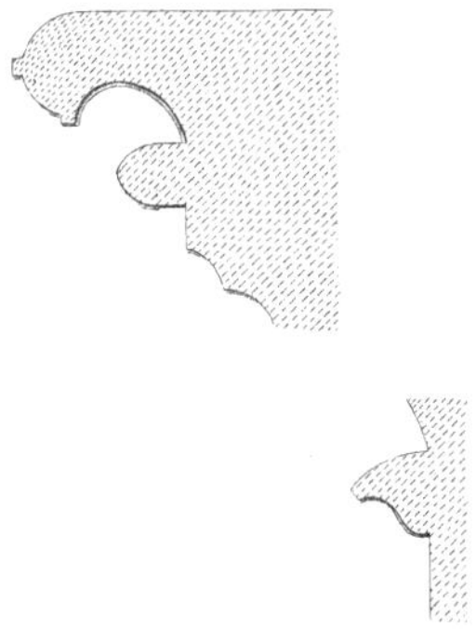

Front of the Flowers.

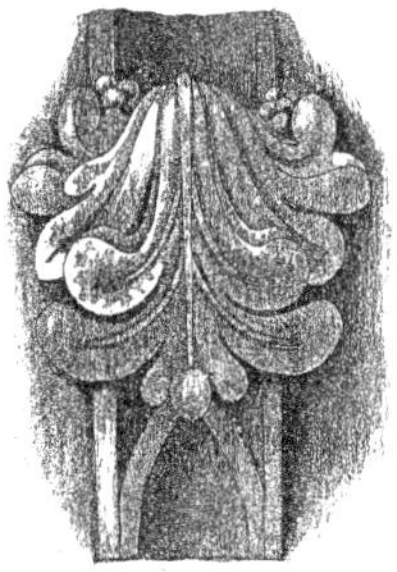

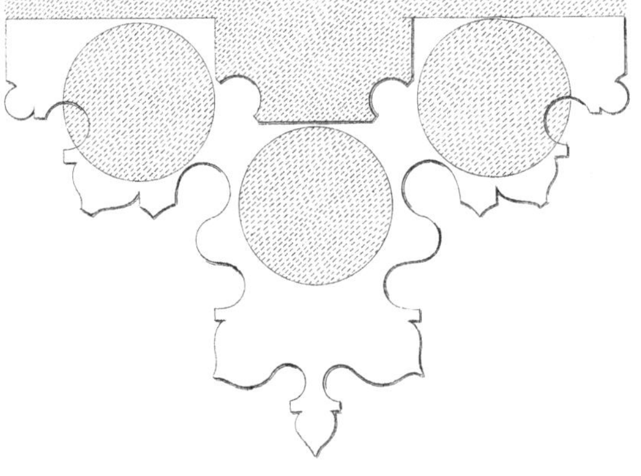

From the Lady Chapel, Lincoln Cathedral.

Date the latter part of the 13th Century.

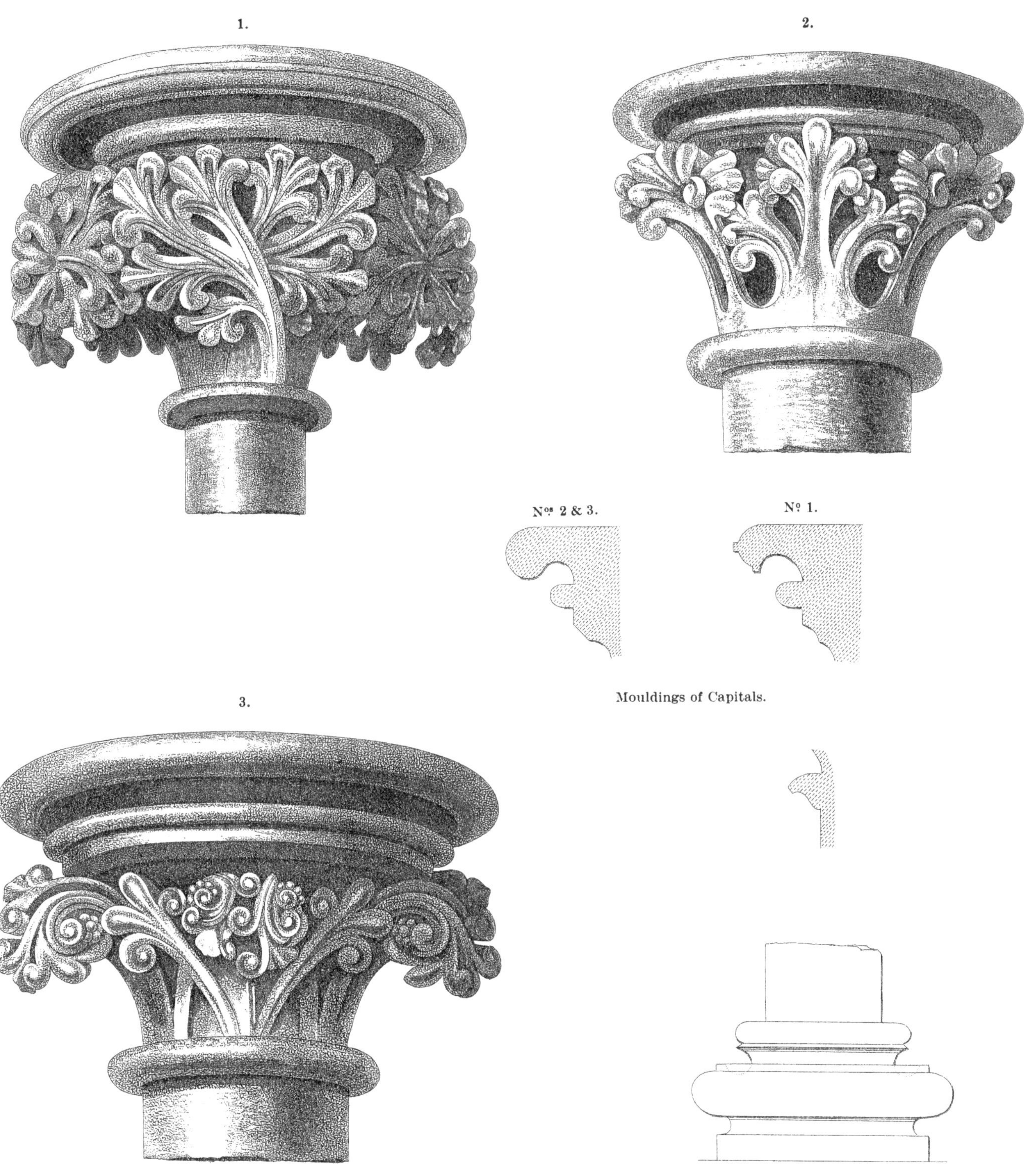

No 1. From Lincoln Cathedral. Nos 2 & 3. From the Library & Chapter Room, Southwell Church, Notts.

Drawn by Henry Shaw.

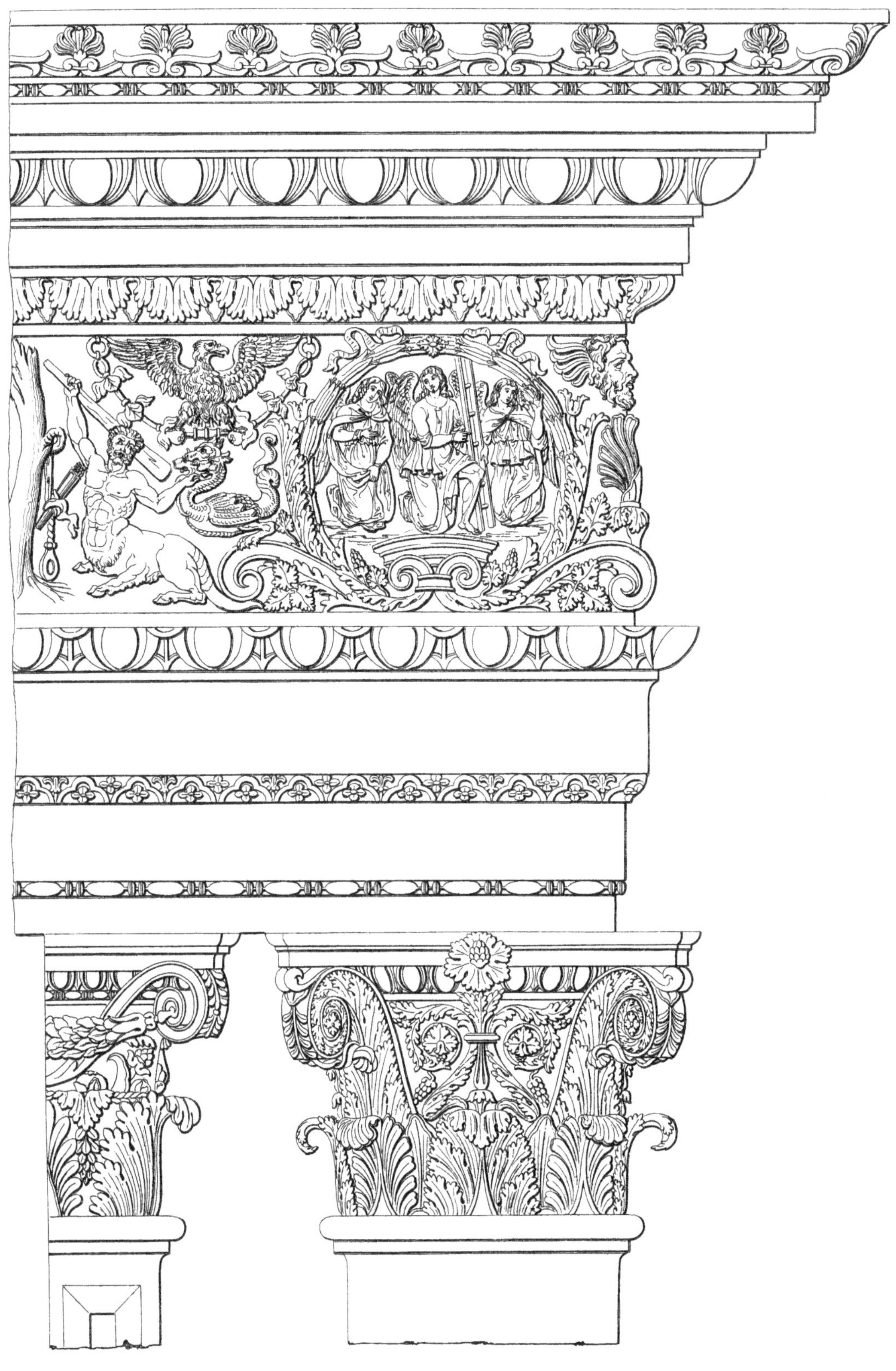

CAPITALS AND ENTABLATURE IN MARBLE,

from the Facade of the Certosa di Pavia.

Date the beginning of the 16th Century.

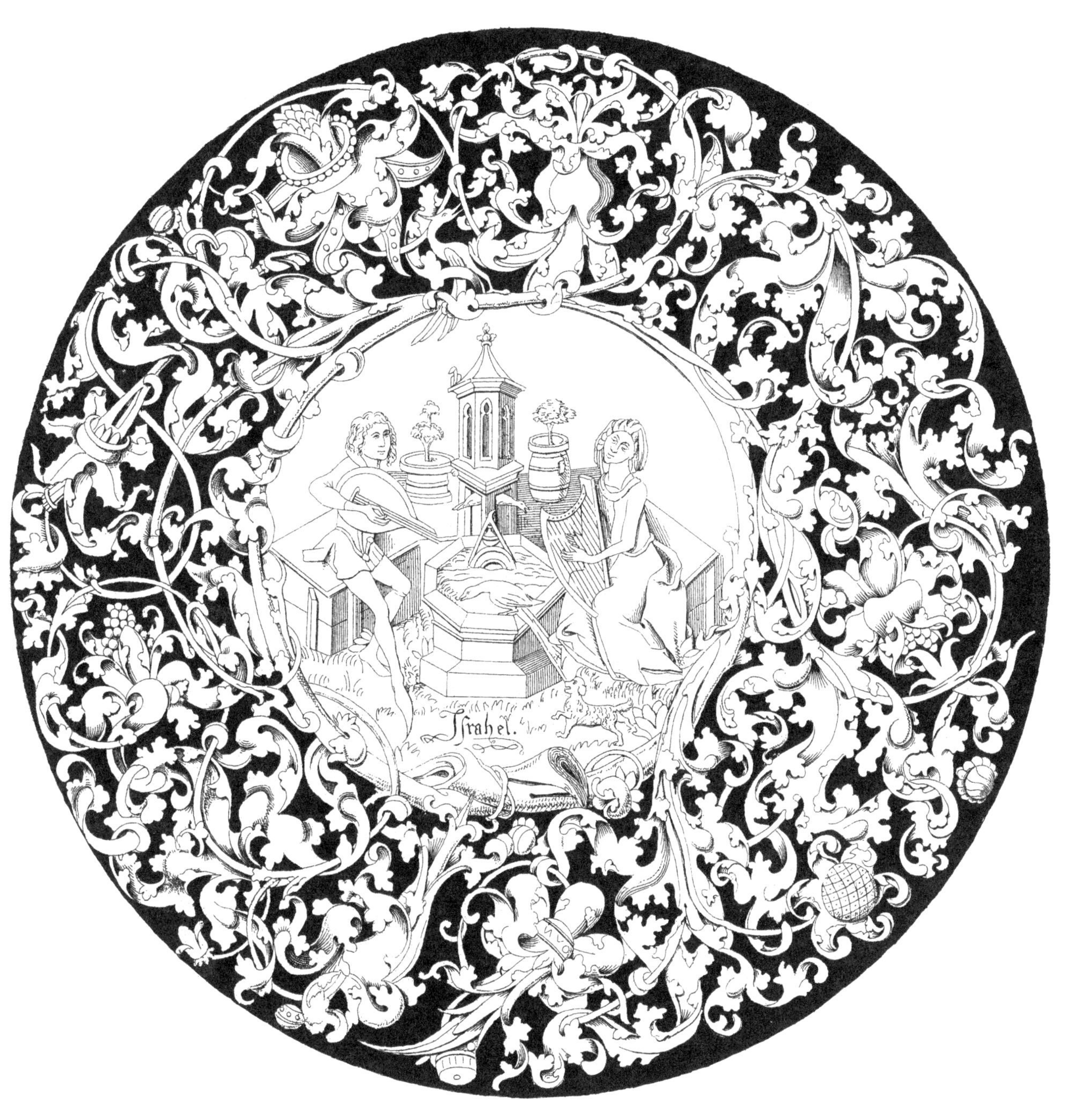

From an Engraving by Israel Van Meeken. Born . Died 1503.

Date 1570.

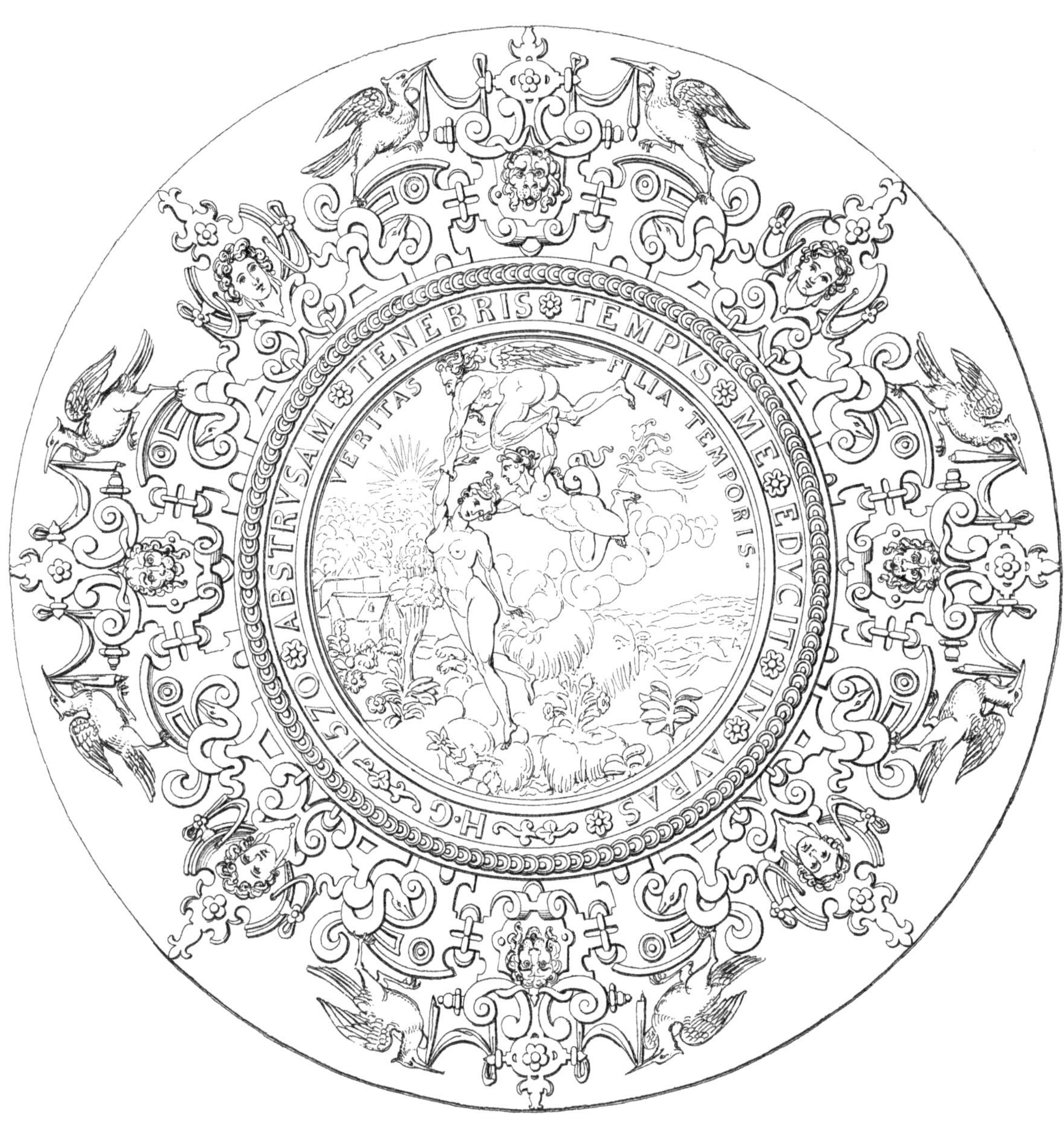

SAME SIZE AS THE ORIGINAL IN METAL,

From the Collection of Thos Willement, F.S.A.

Drawn & Engraved by Henry Shaw.

Date the beginning of the 16th Century.

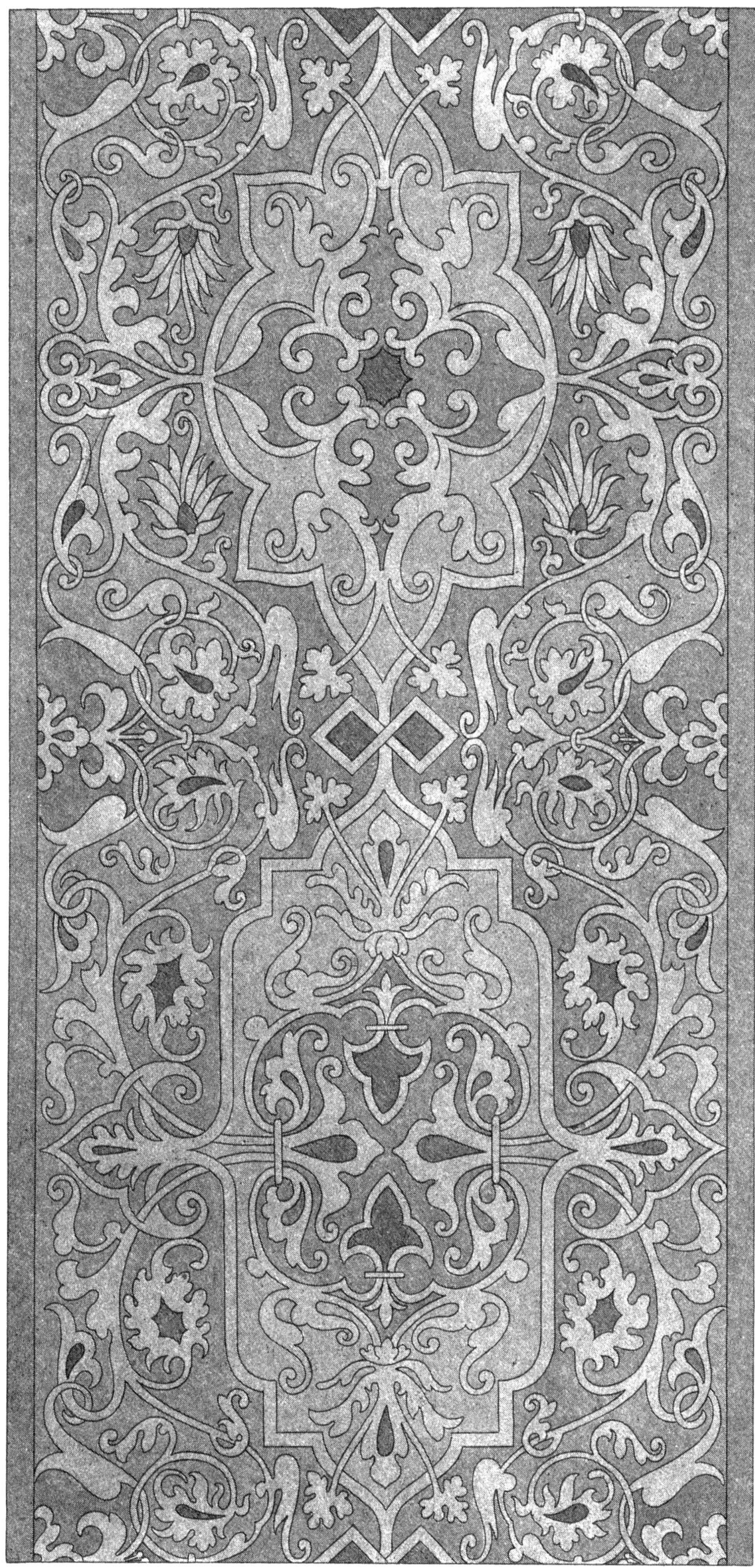

DRAPERY,

From a Picture in the Louvre.

by Cima da Conegliano.

½ size.

Date the beginning of the 17th Century.

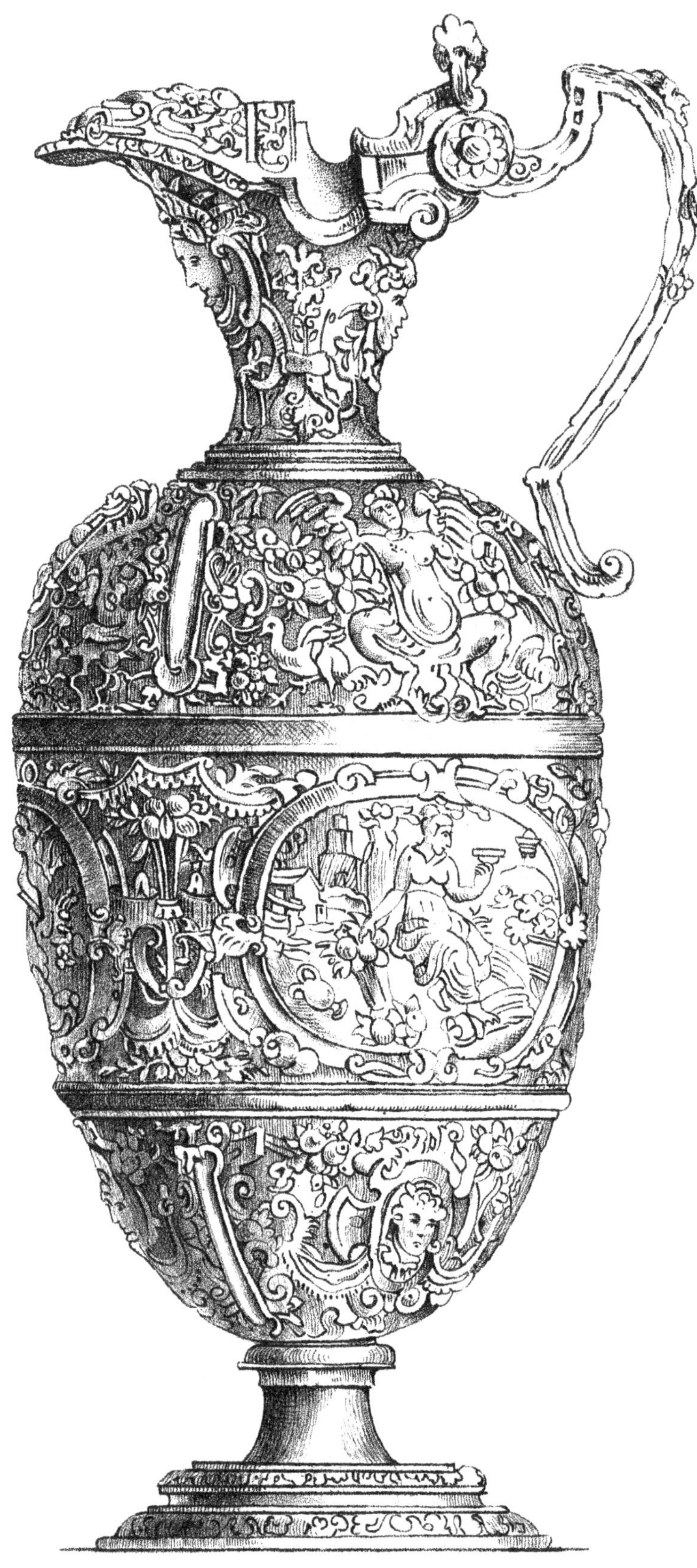

JAS ANDREWS ZINCO

EWER.

From the Collection of Monsr. Trisson Languedoc.

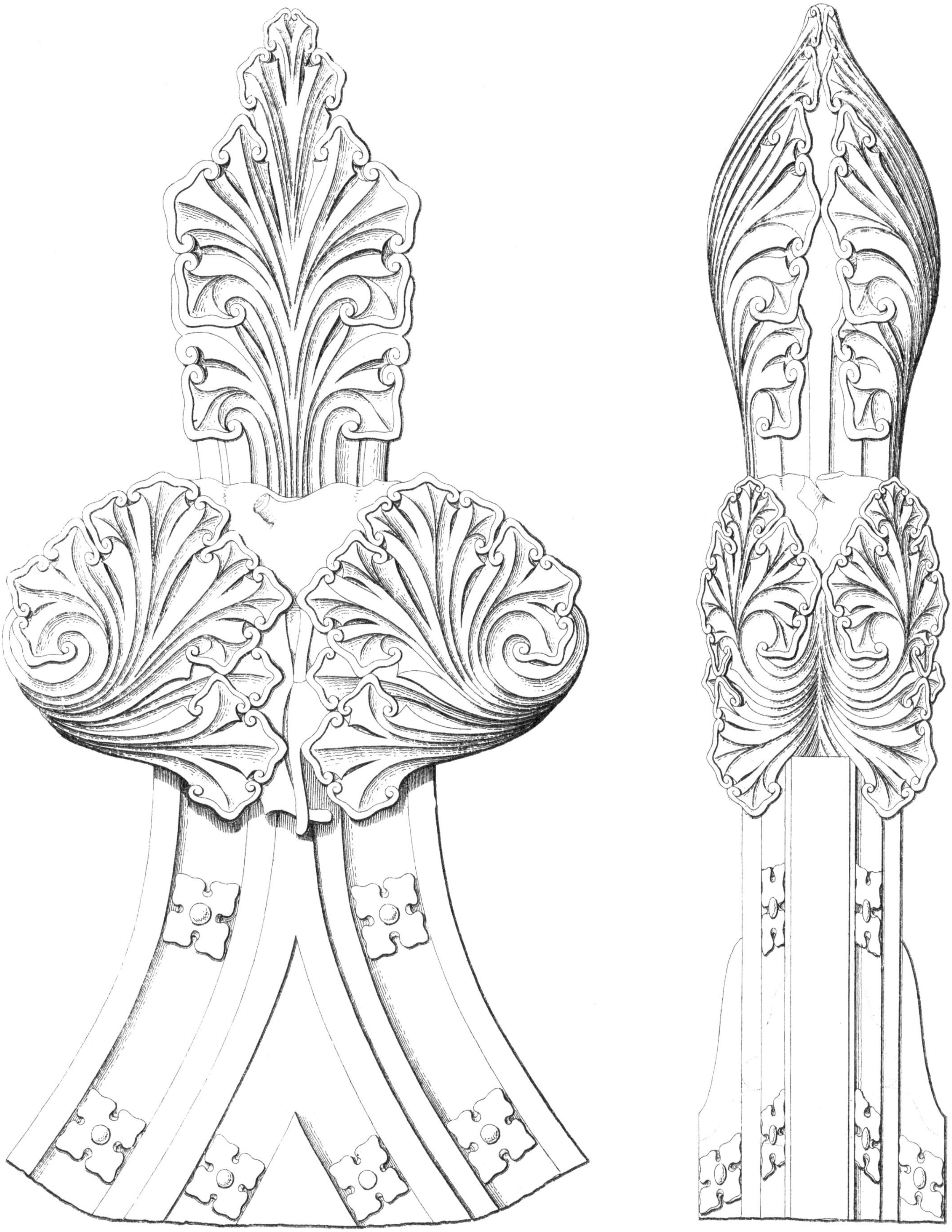

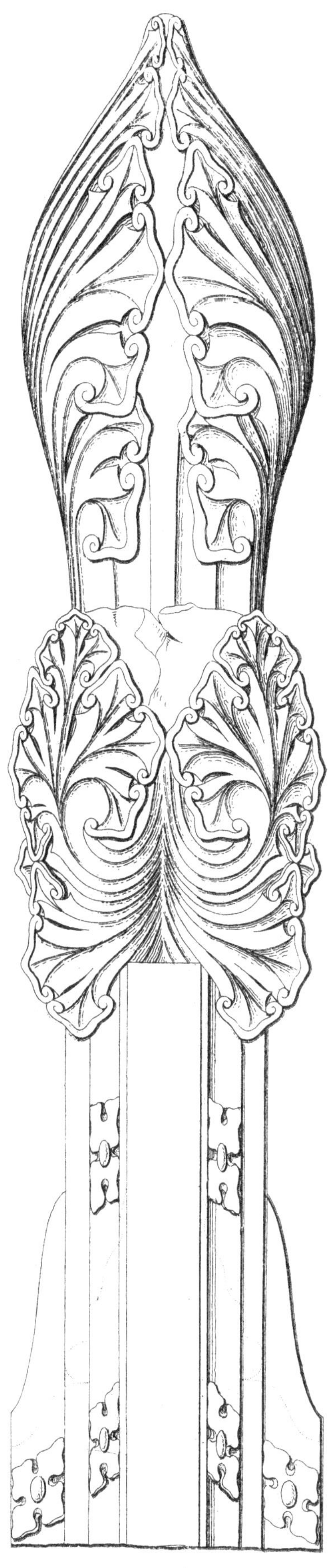

A FINIAL.

From Lincoln Cathedral.

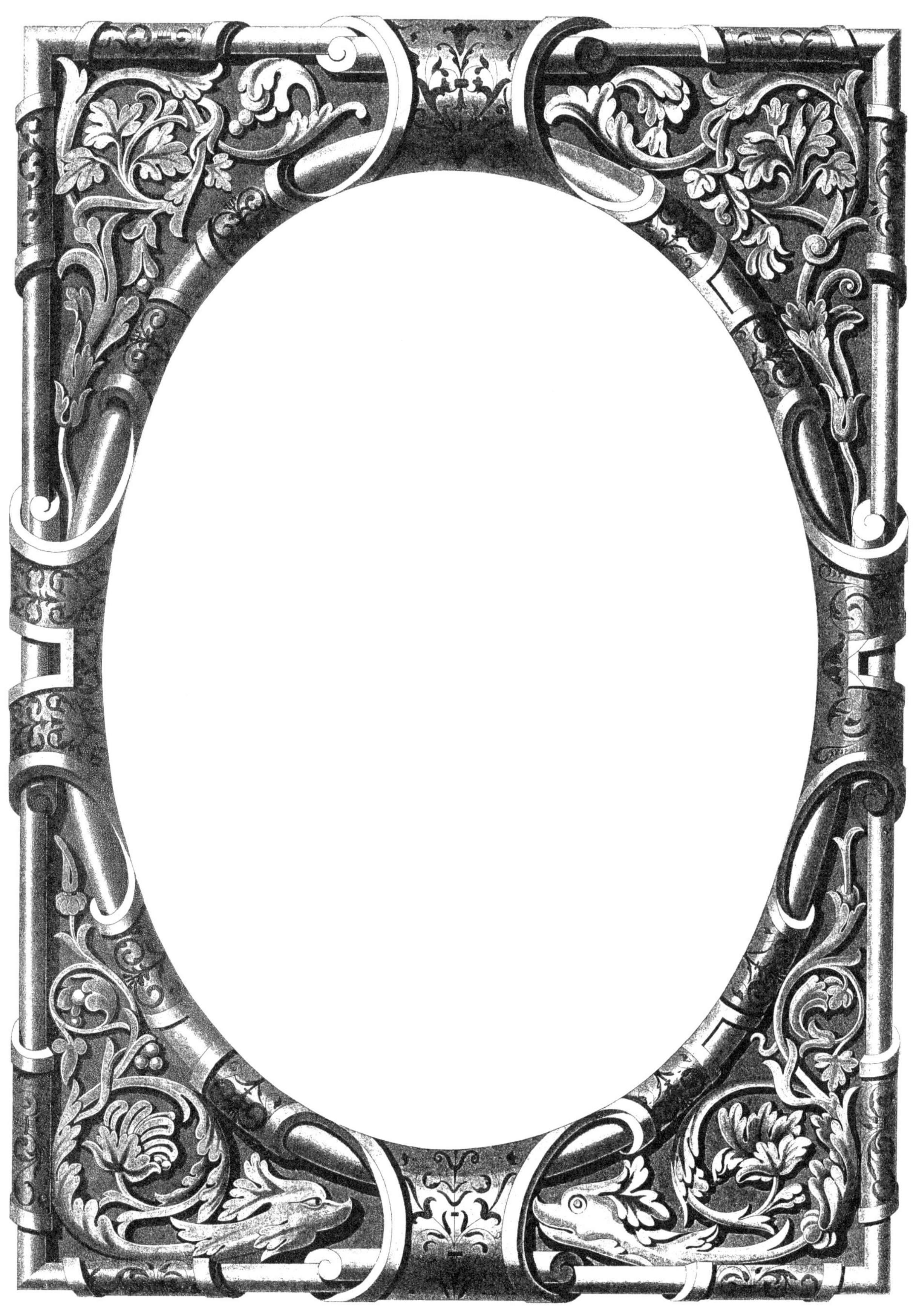

FROM A DRAWING

in a M.S. in the British Museum.

Royal M.S. II. D. 40.

Date the beginning of the 16th Century.

Date the time of Henry 8th

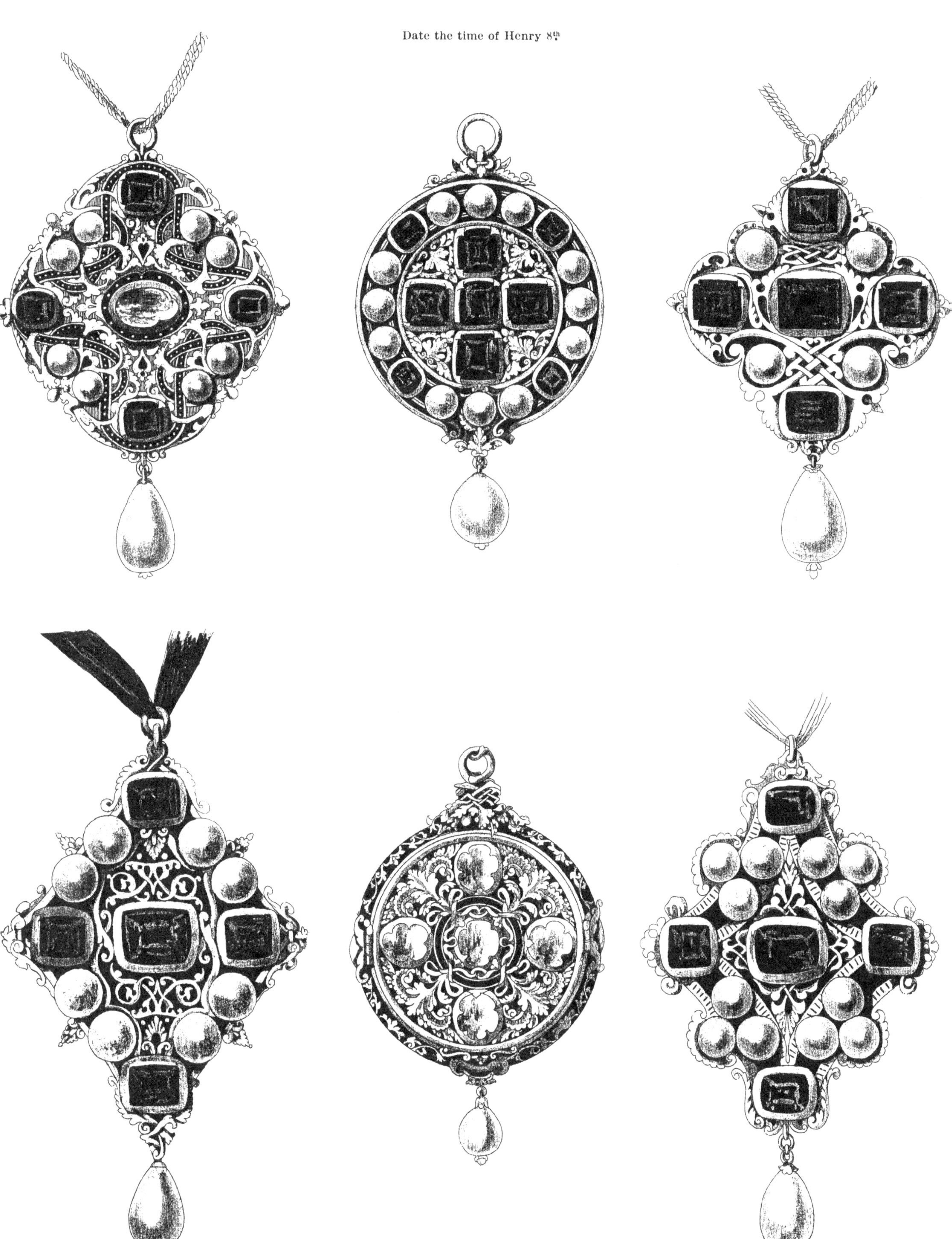

DESIGNS FOR GOLDSMITHS WORK

by Hans Holbein.

In the British Museum. Additional M.S. 5308.

Date time of Henry 8th

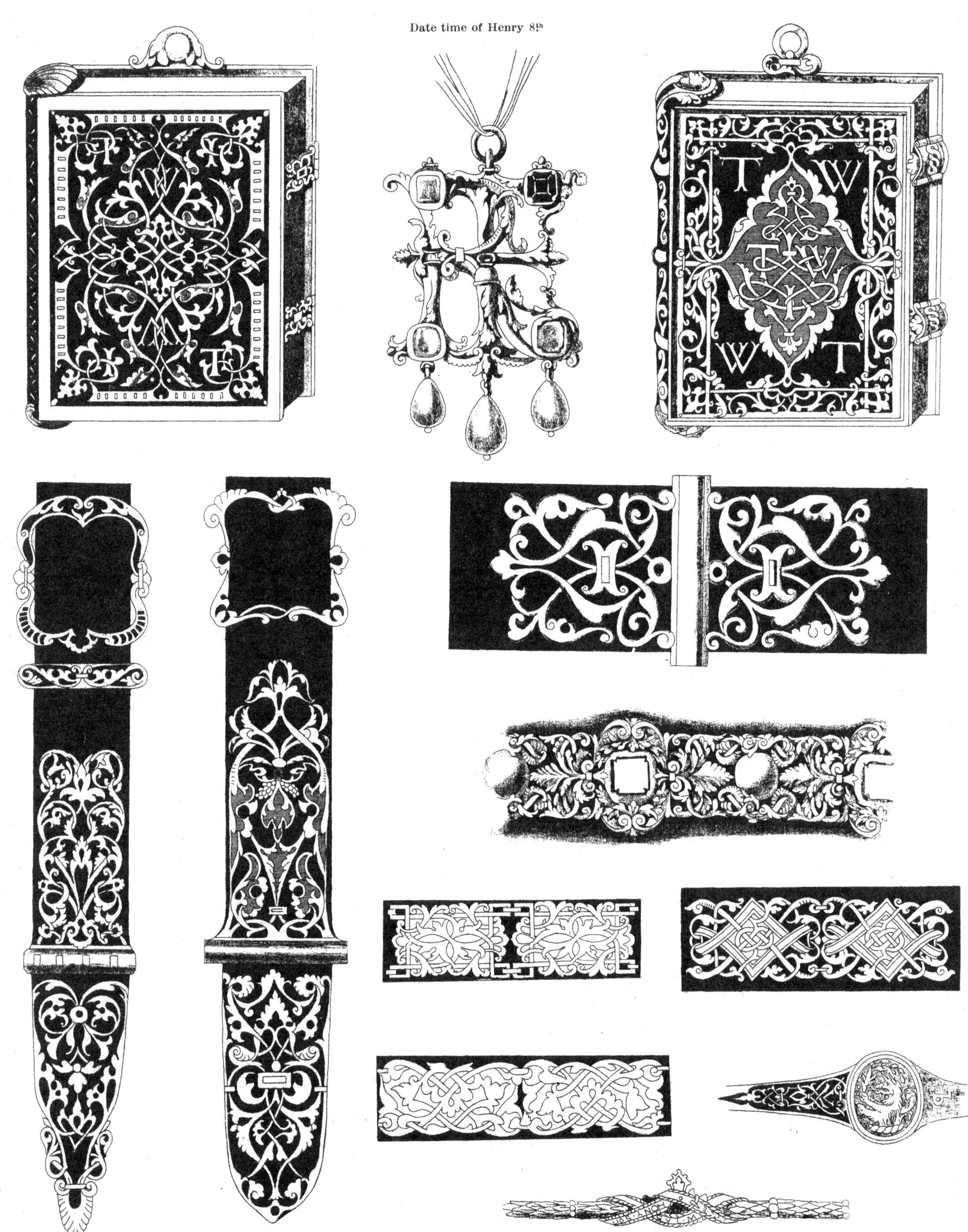

DESIGNS FOR GOLDSMITHS WORK,

by Hans Holbein.

In the British Museum. Additional M.S. 5308.

Date the 16th Century.

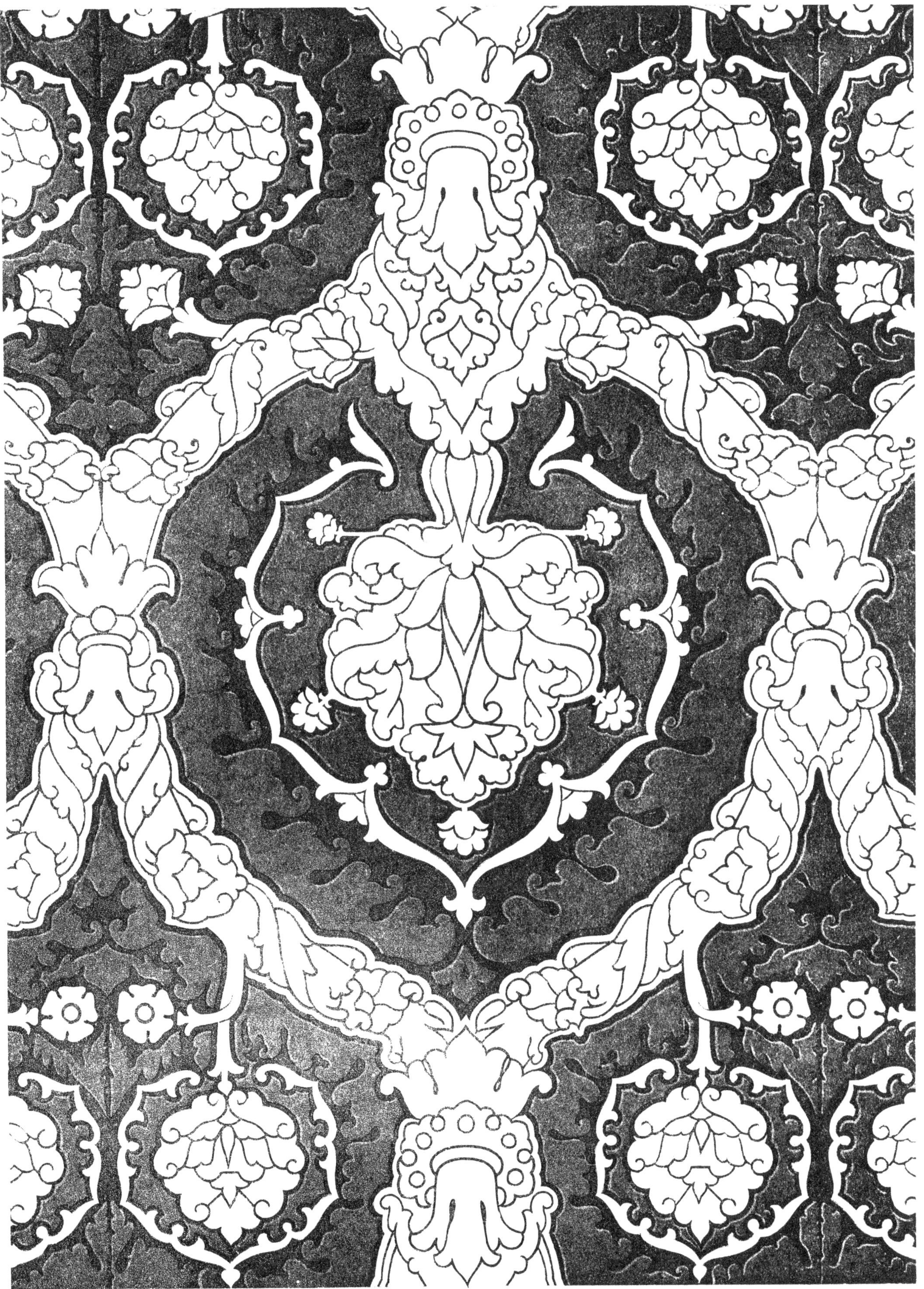

VELVET HANGINGS

Date the end of the 16th Century.

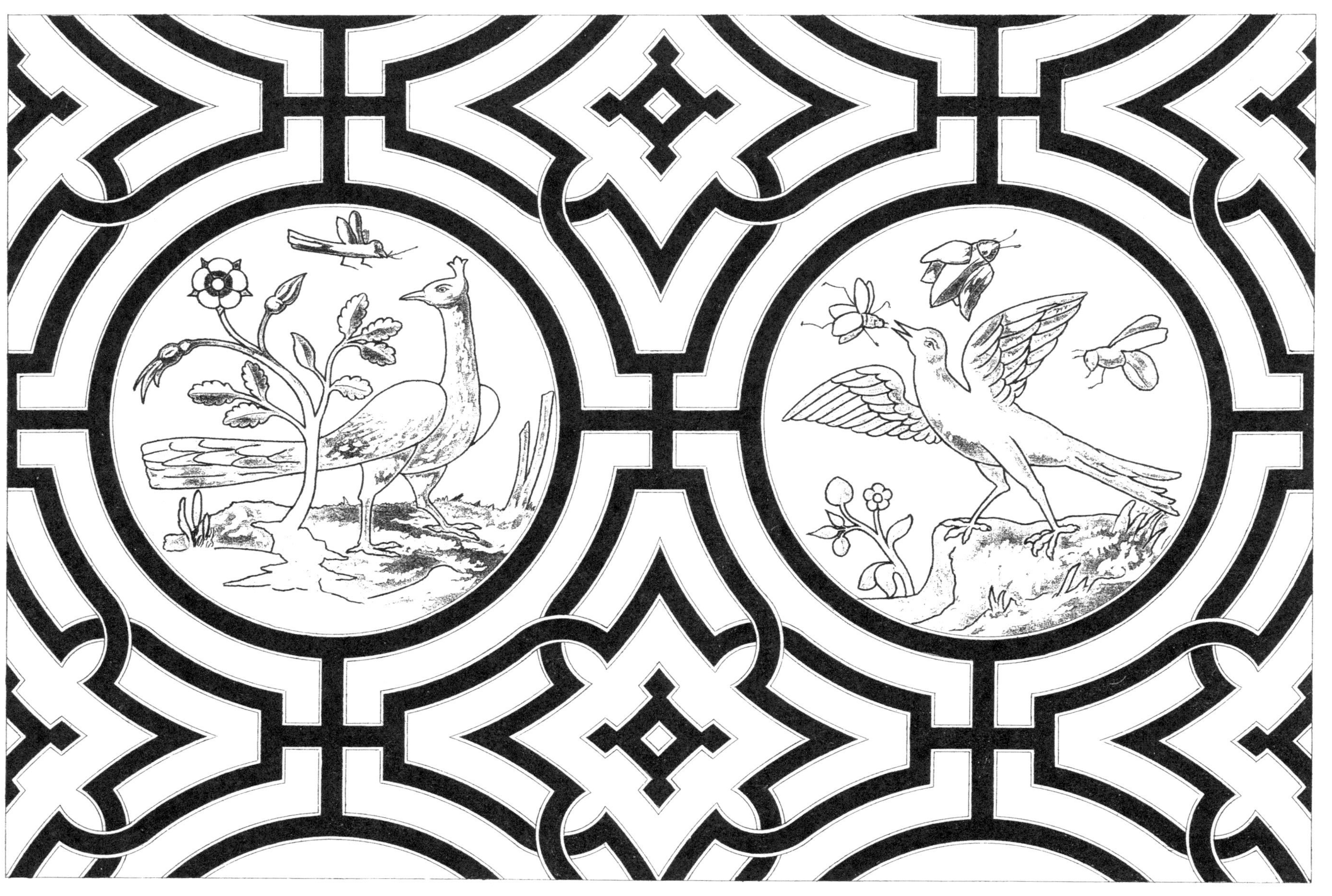

FROM VELVET HANGINGS,

at Hardwicke Hall, Derbyshire.

Date the 13th Century.

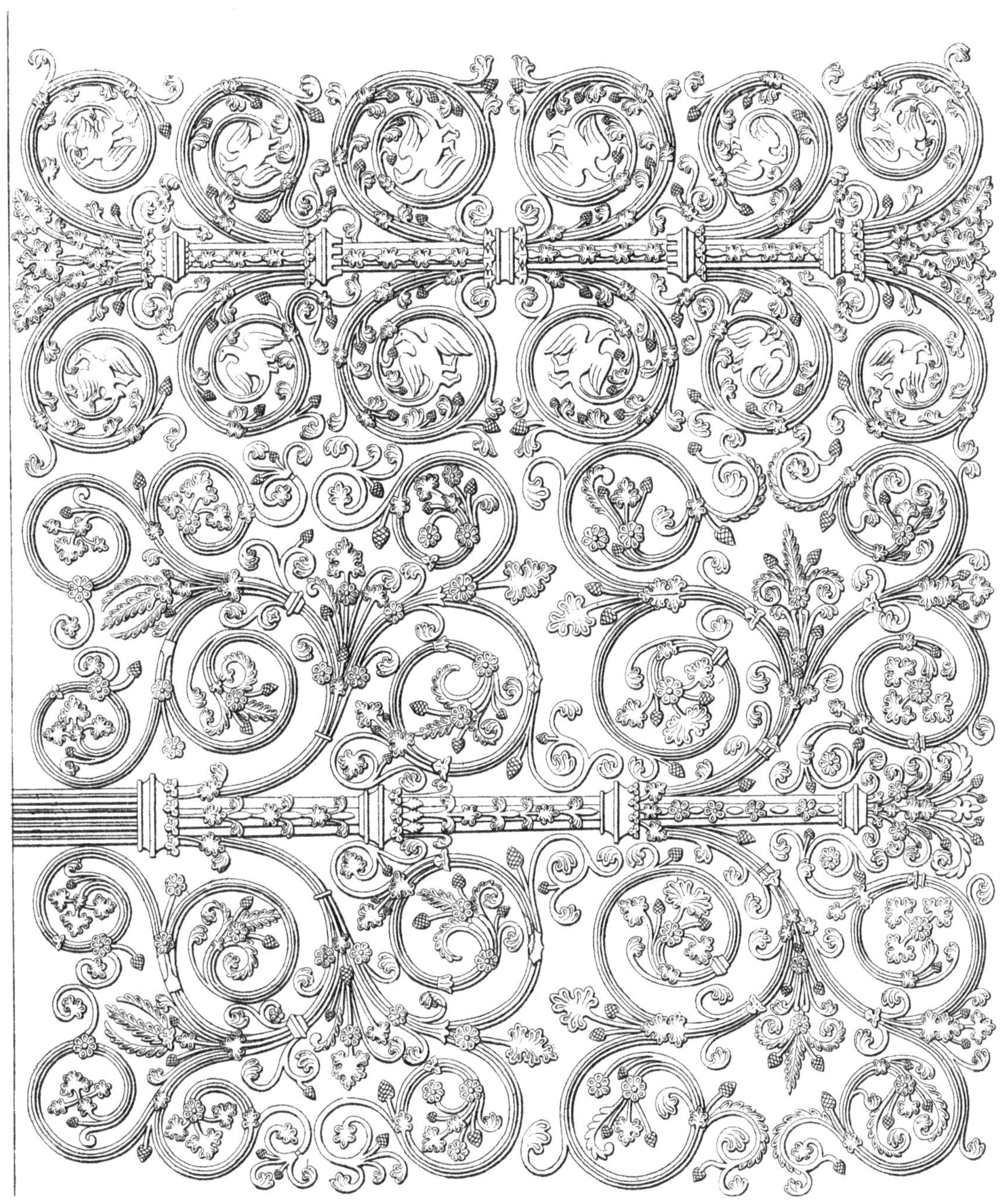

IRON WORK.

From the Door of Notre Dame Cathedral, Paris.

H. Shaw.

Date 1518.

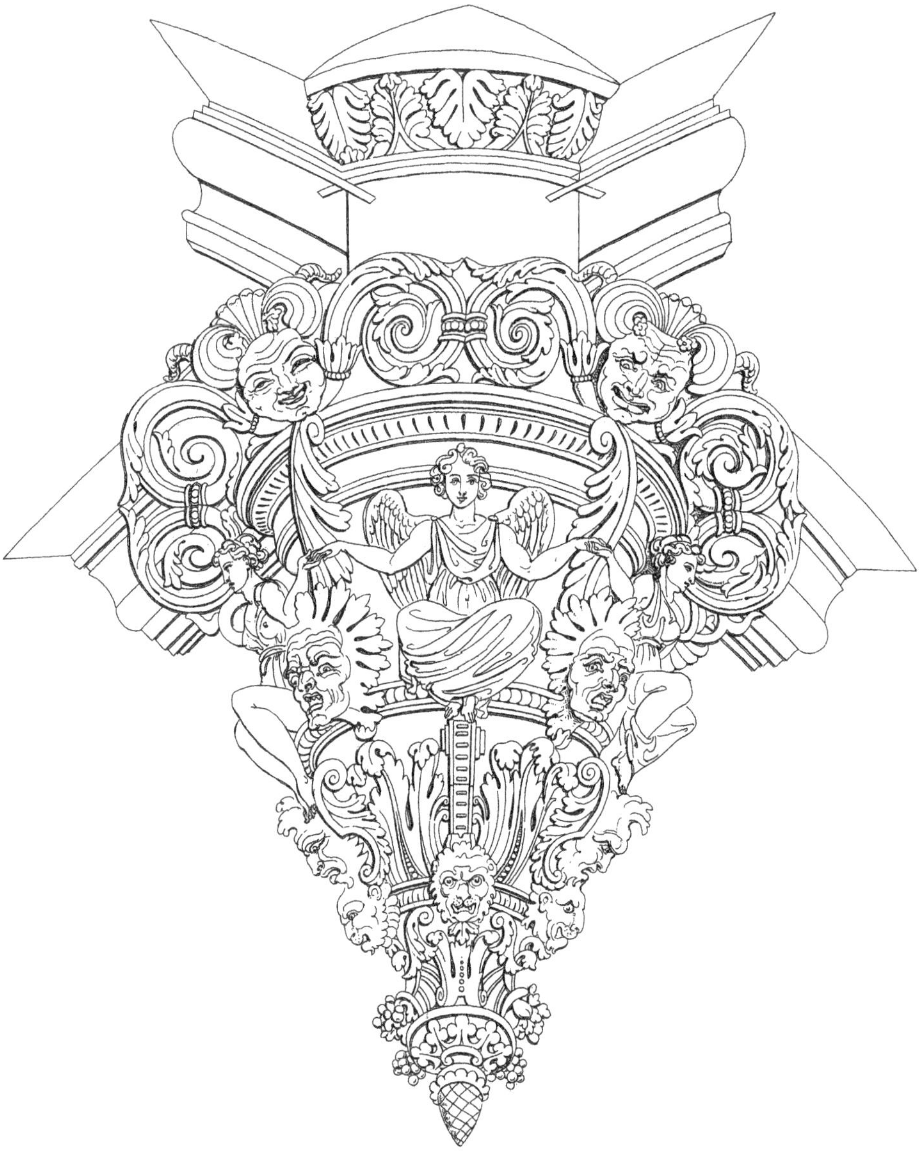

KEY STONE & ORNAMENTS

round a capital in the Church of

Pont de l'arche, Normandy.

Date 1601.

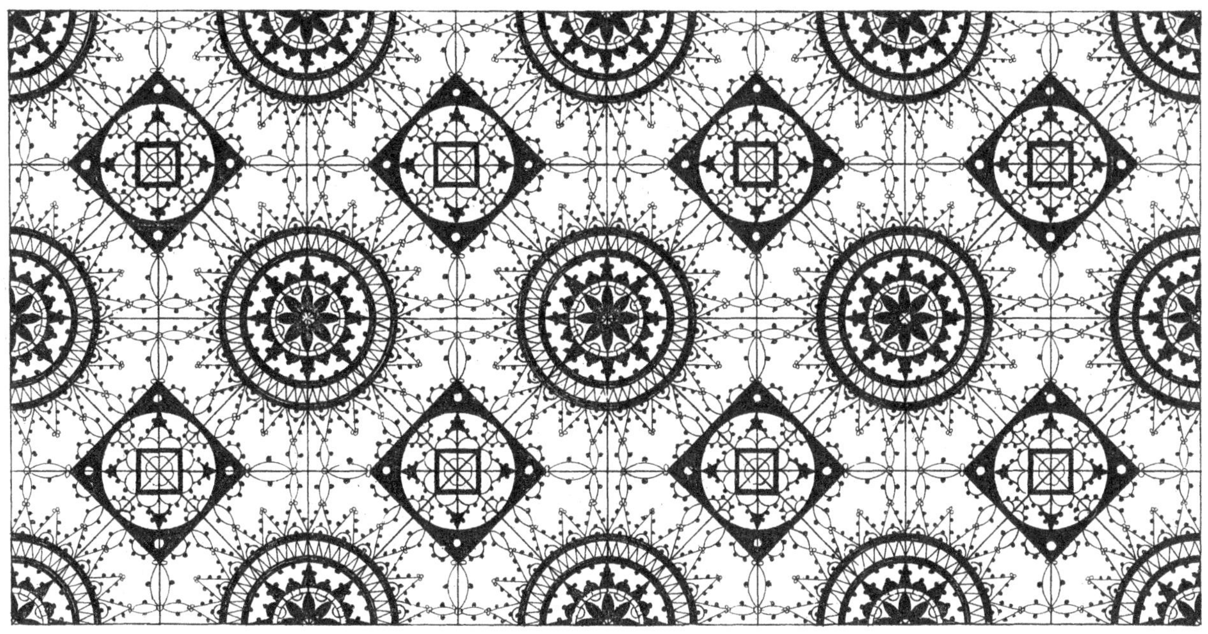

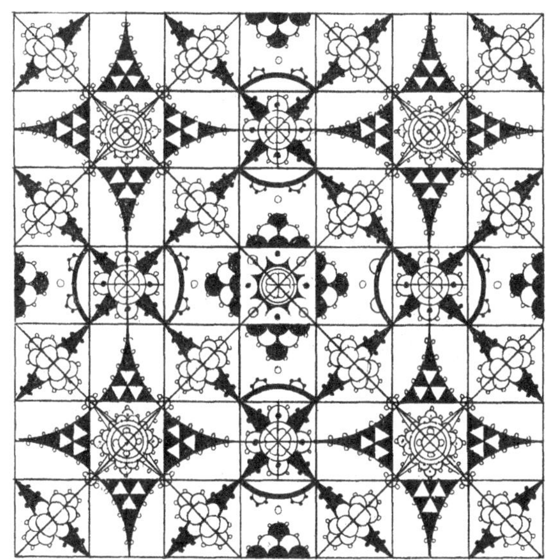

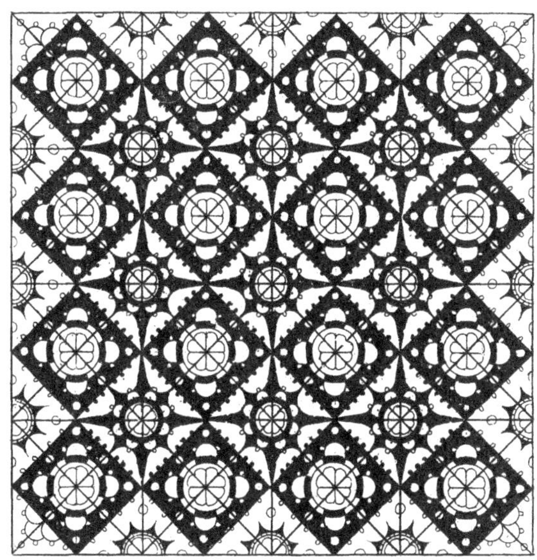

ANCIENT LACE WORK.

Date 1601.

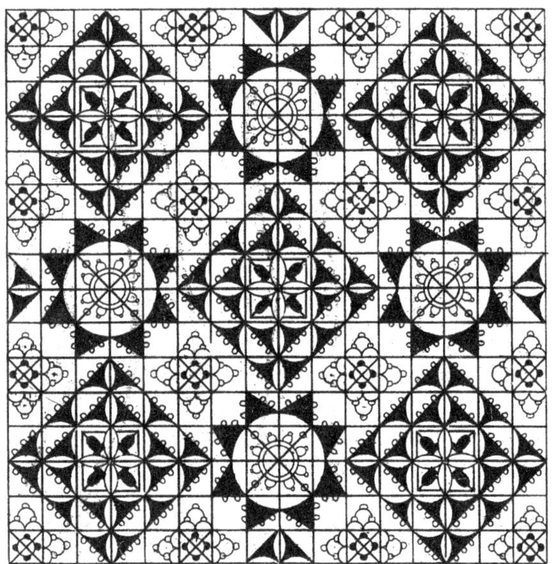

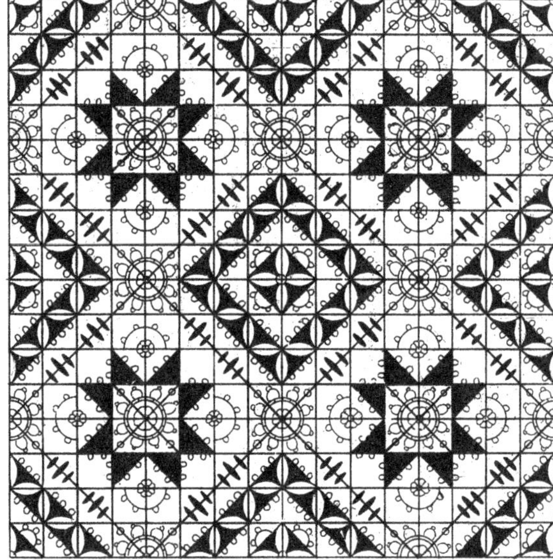

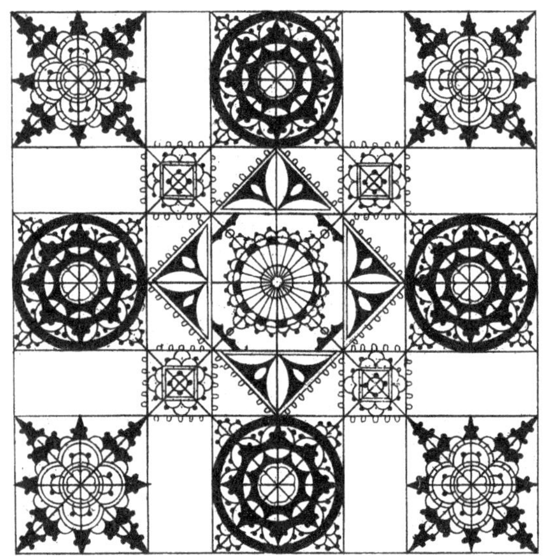

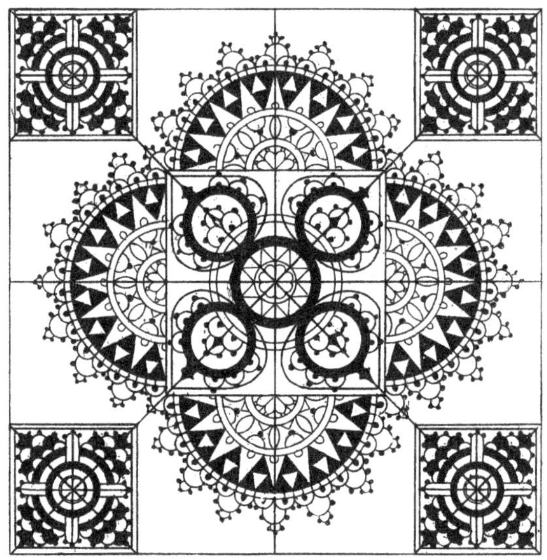

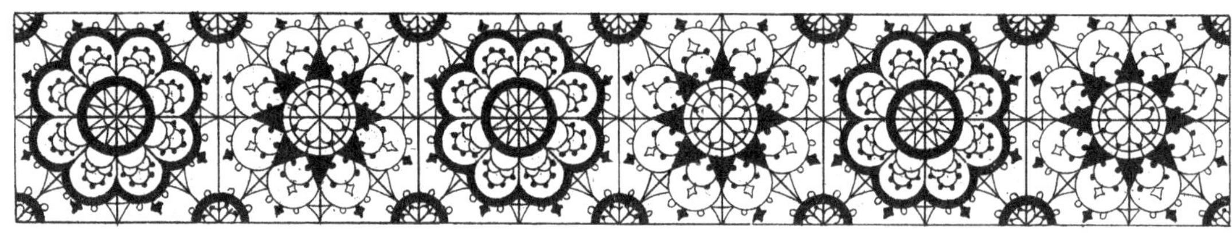

ANCIENT LACE WORK.

NEEDLEWORK.

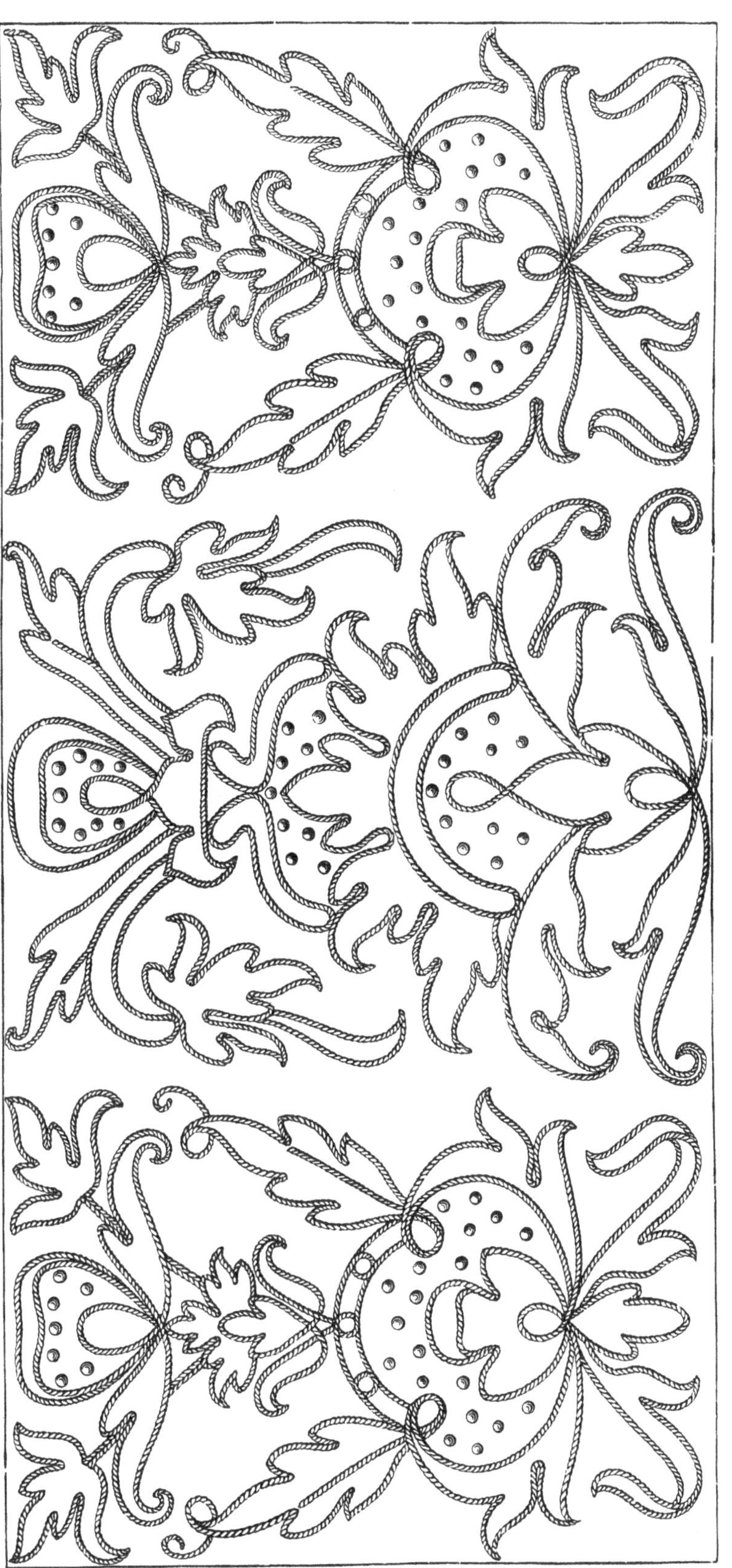

About 1650.

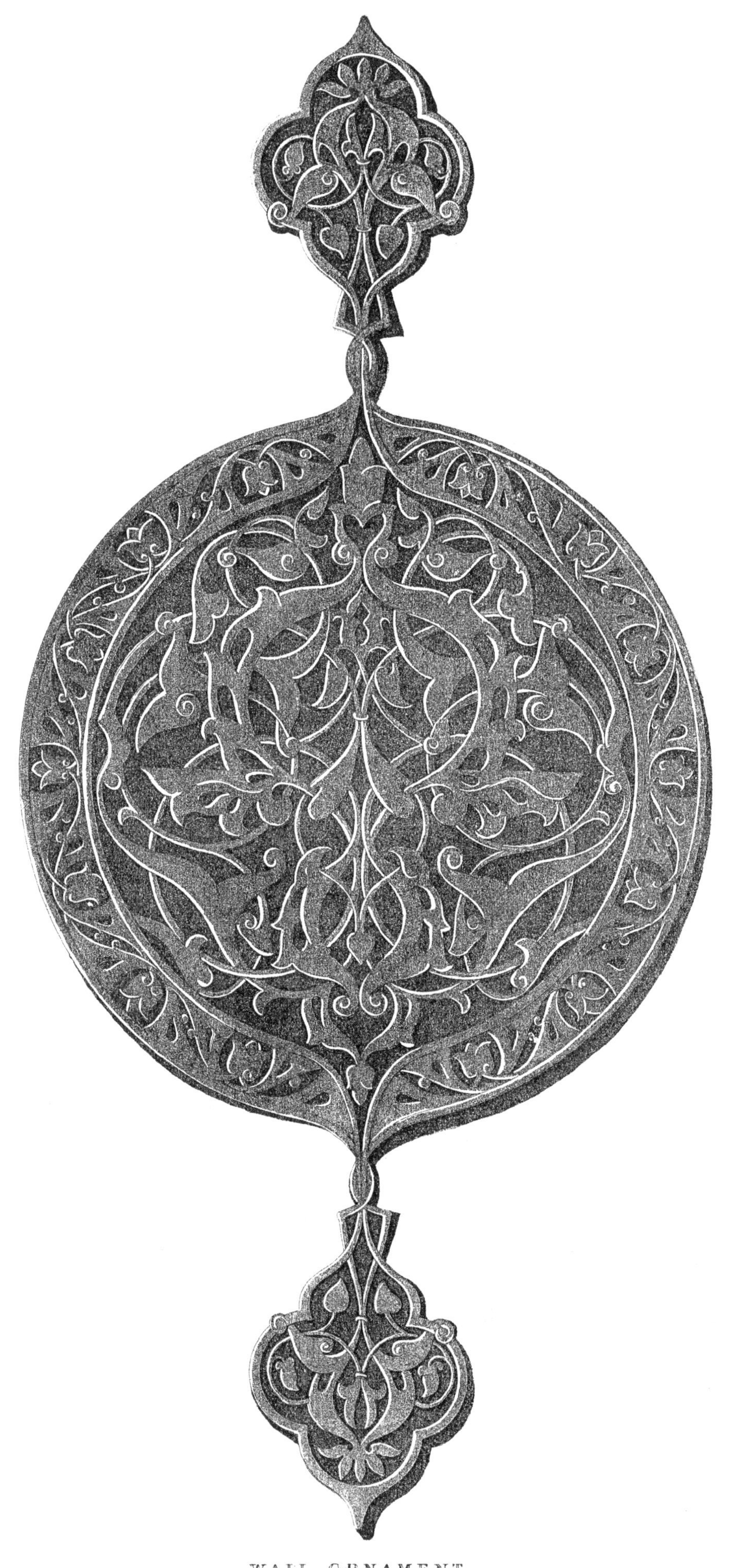

WALL ORNAMENT

on the Tomb of Ibrahim Aga in Cairo.

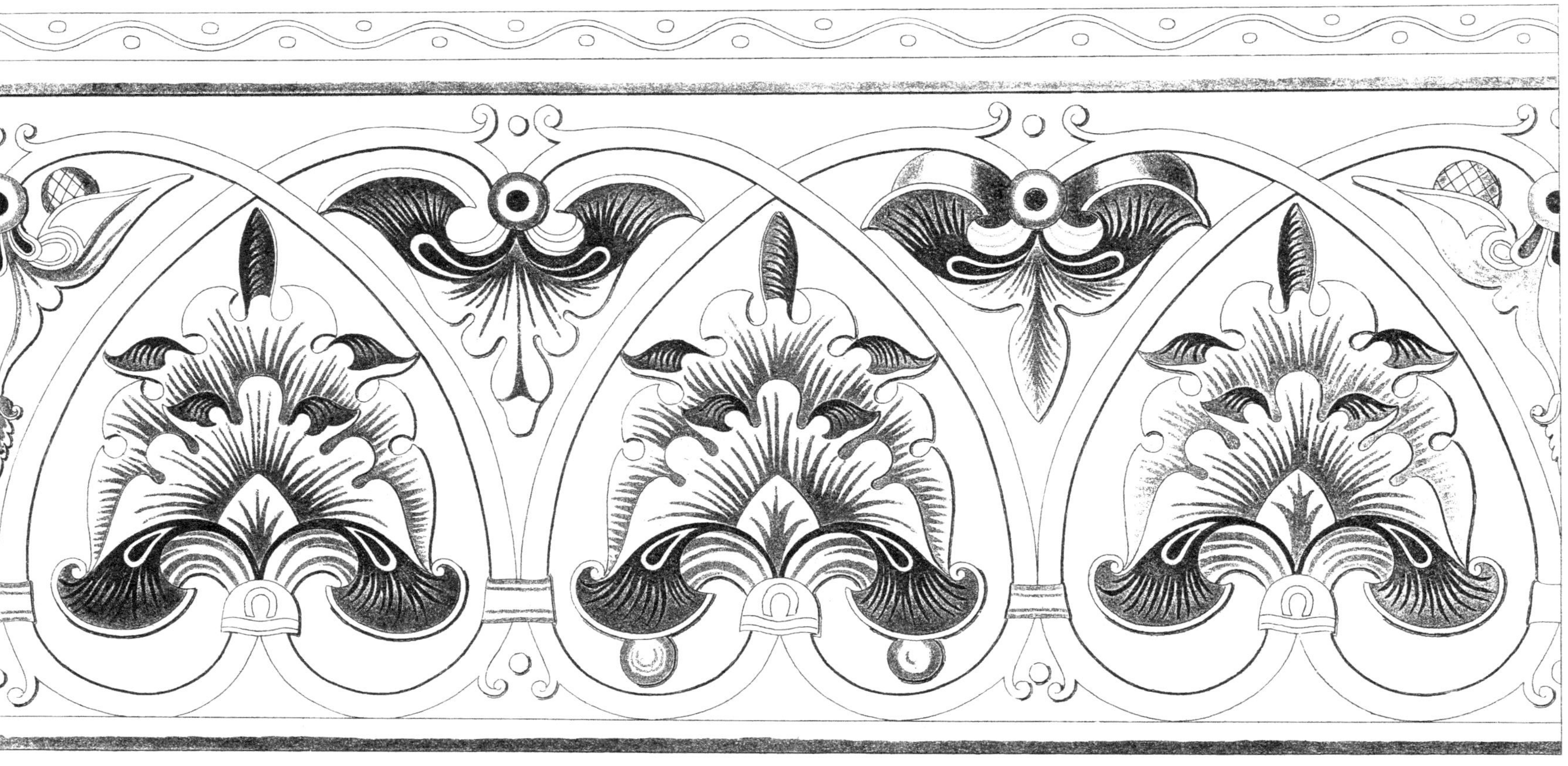

ORNAMENT,

From the Gallilee of Durham Cathedral.

Date the end of the 12th Century.

Date the beginning of the 15th Century.

1.

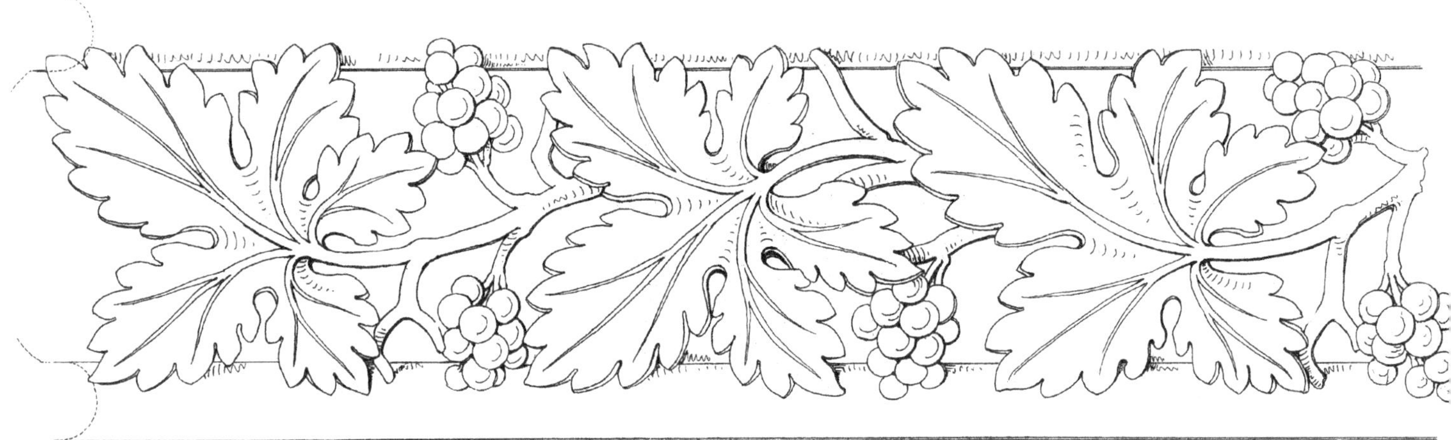

2.

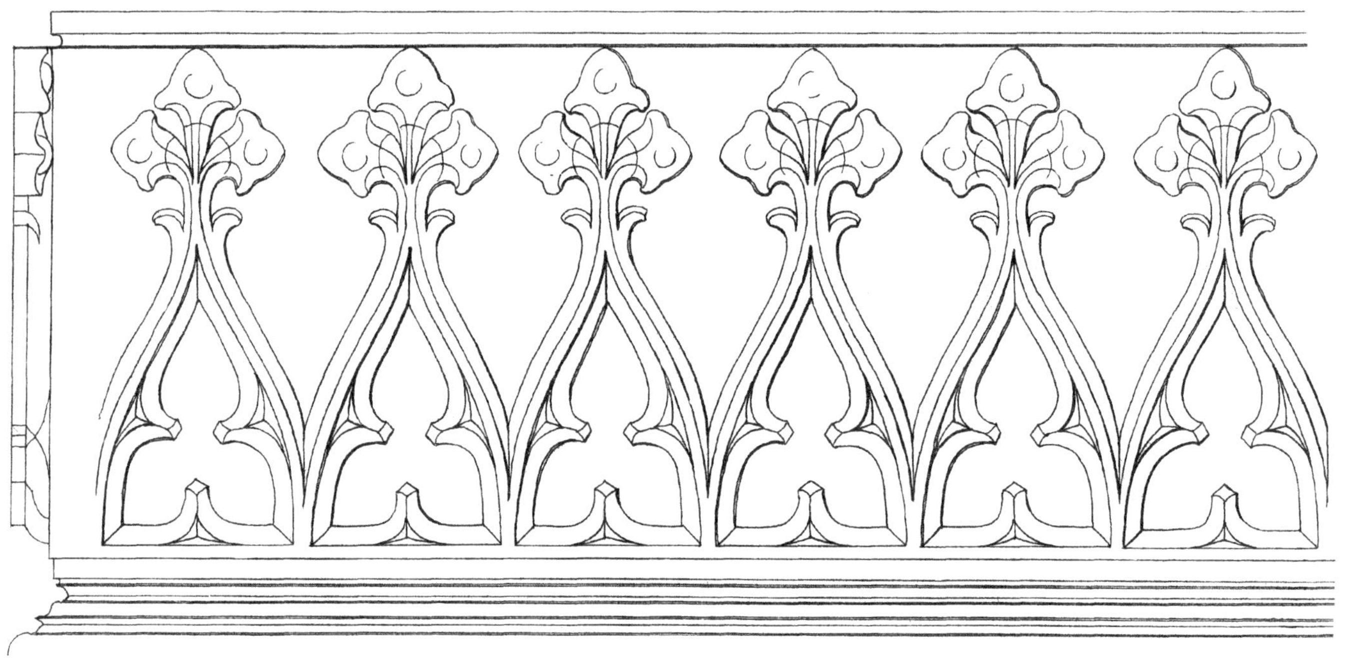

Nº 1. From Southwell Church.—2. From Furneſs Abbey.

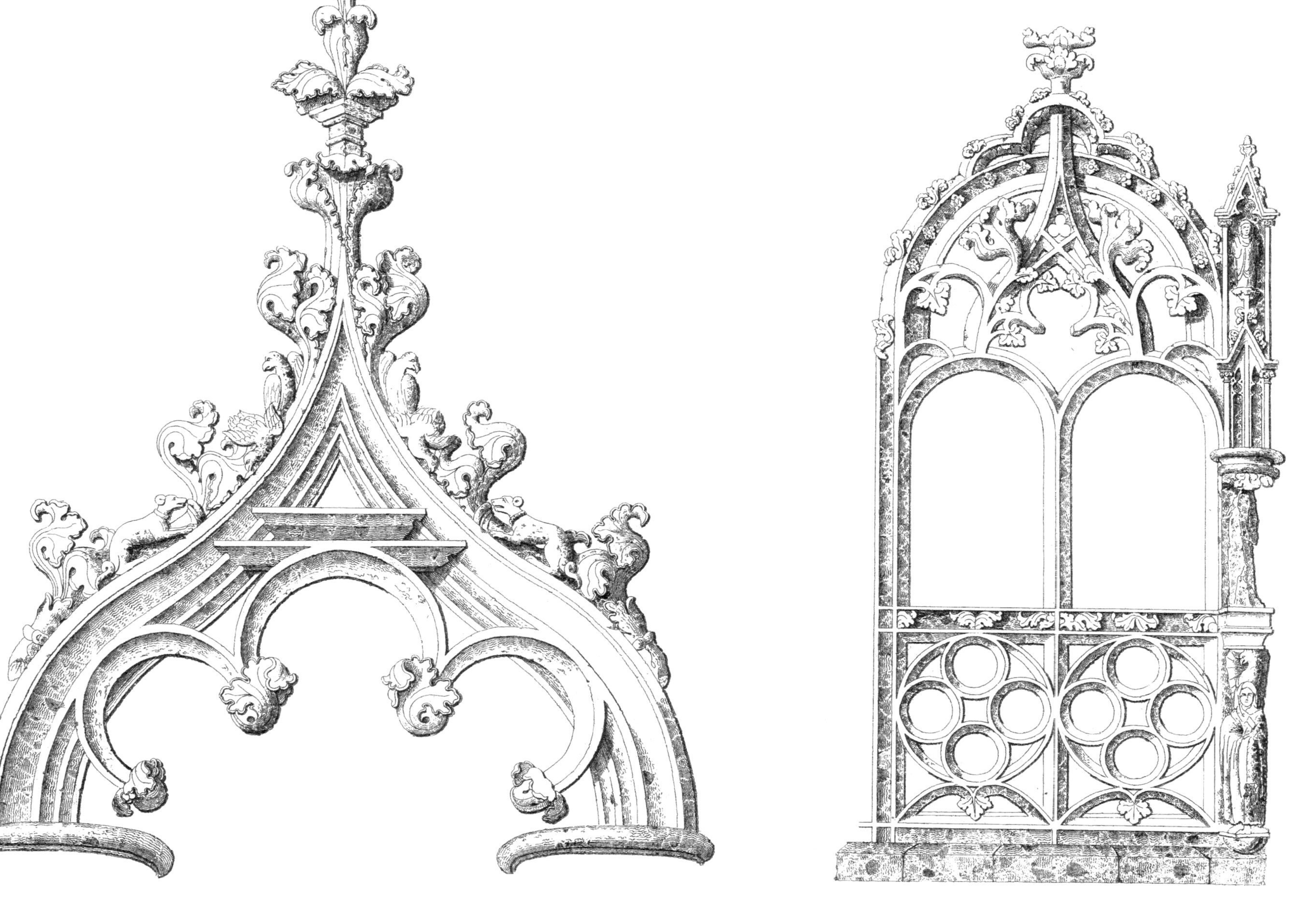

FROM THE ABBEY OF JUMIEGES,

in Normandy.

Date the latter part of the 15th Century.

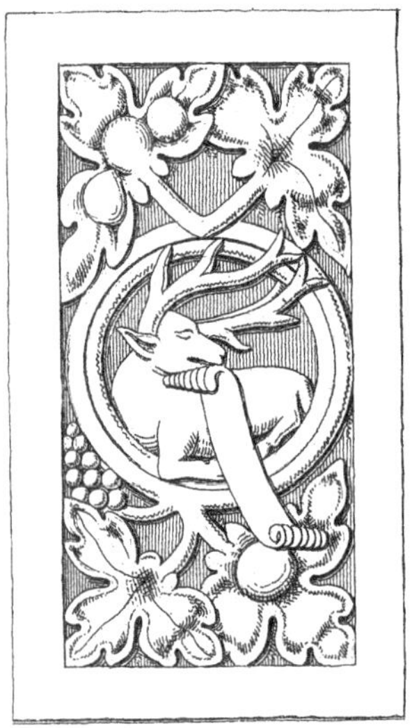
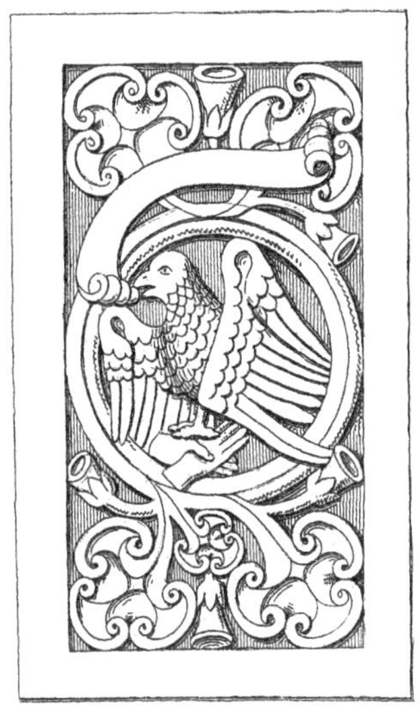
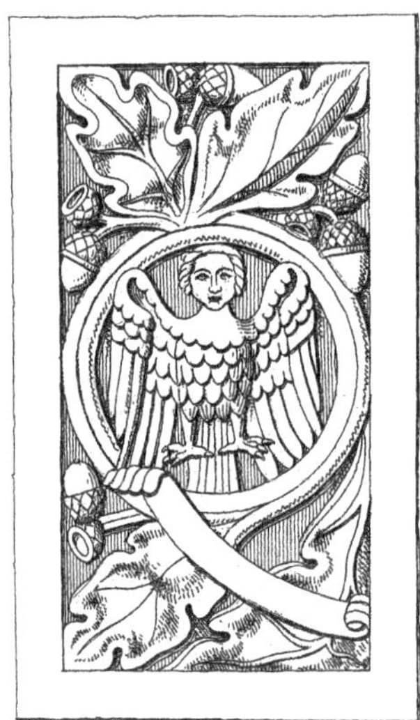
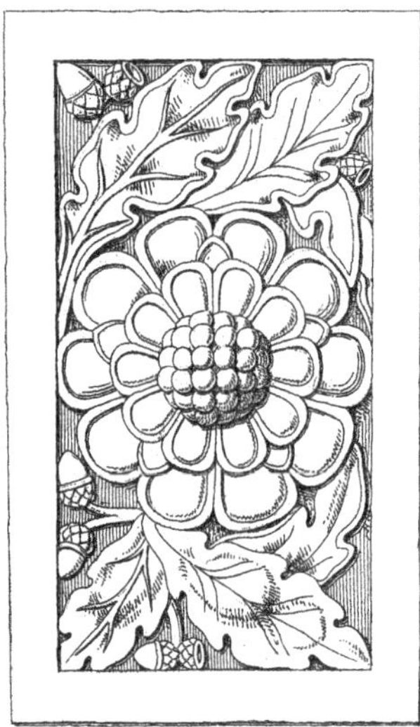

Date the end of the 15th Century.

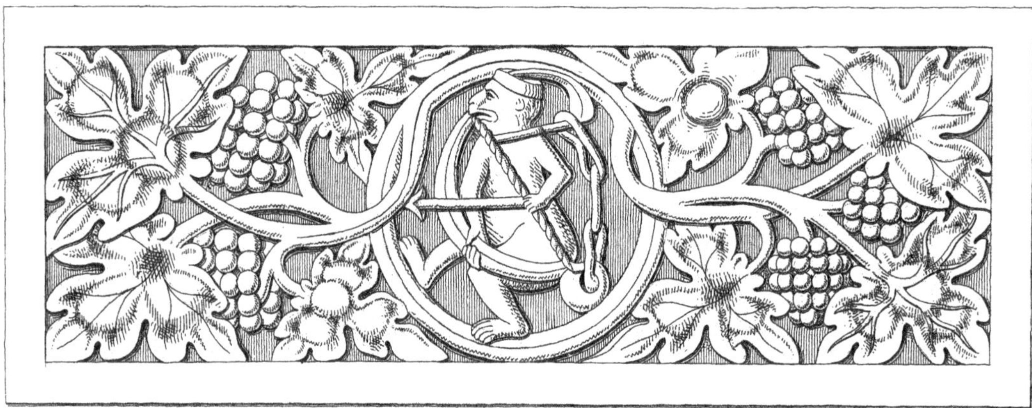

Centre panel ⅔ full size the rest ½.

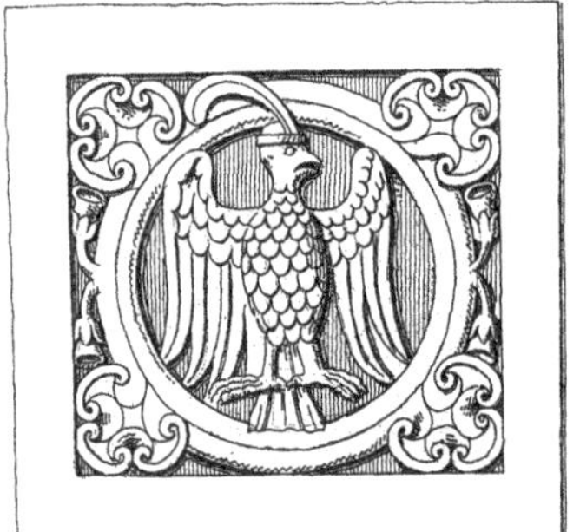
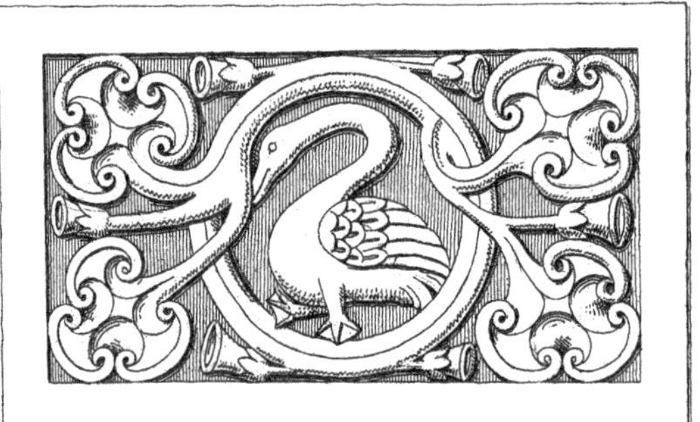
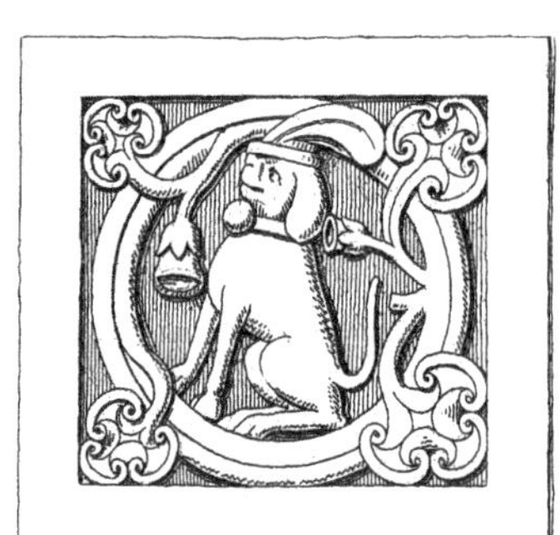

Ornaments on the Box containing the Seal of the

Royal Hospital of St. Catherine, Regent's Park.

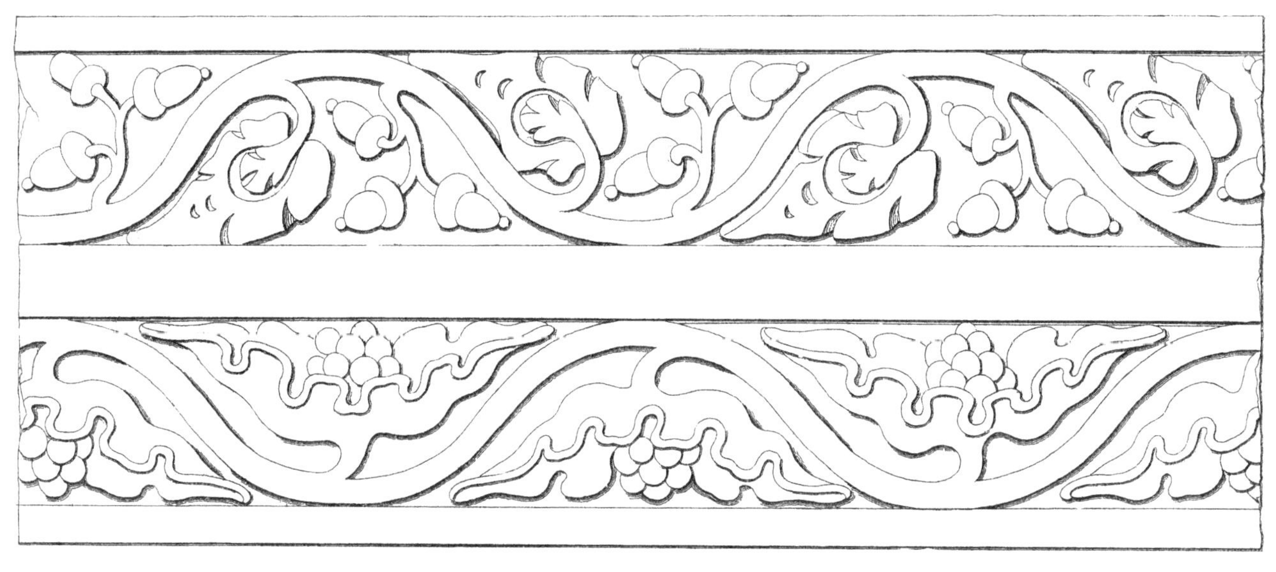

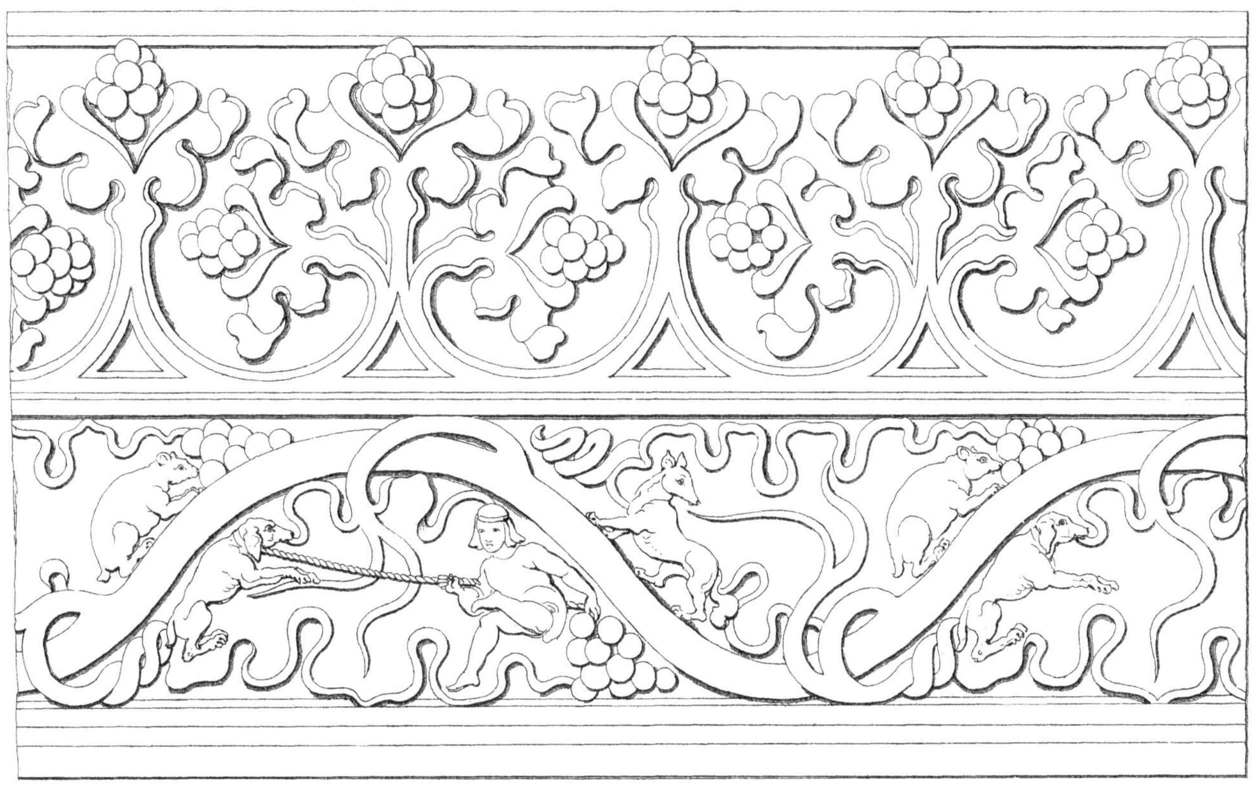

ORNAMENTS ON AN ANCIENT CHAIR,

in St Mary's Hall, Coventry.

Date the latter part of the 15th Century.

⅜ full size.

Date the beginning of the 16th Century.

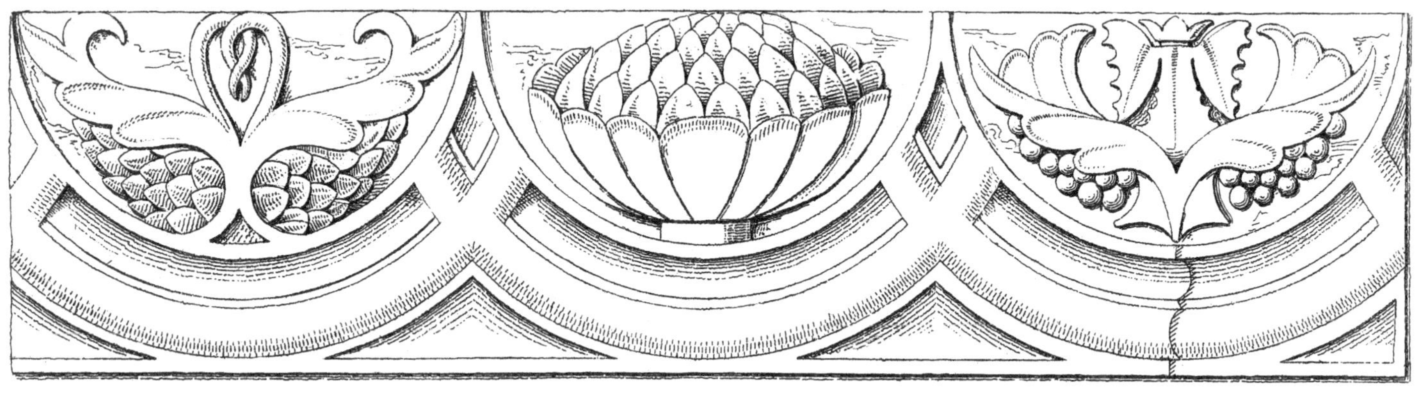

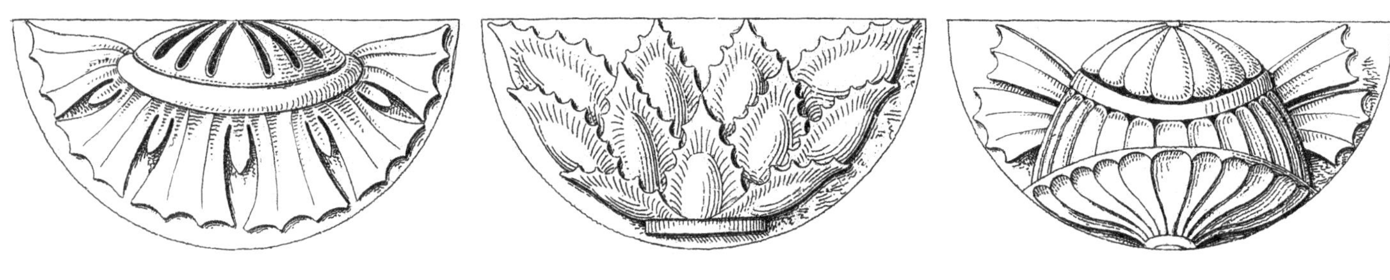

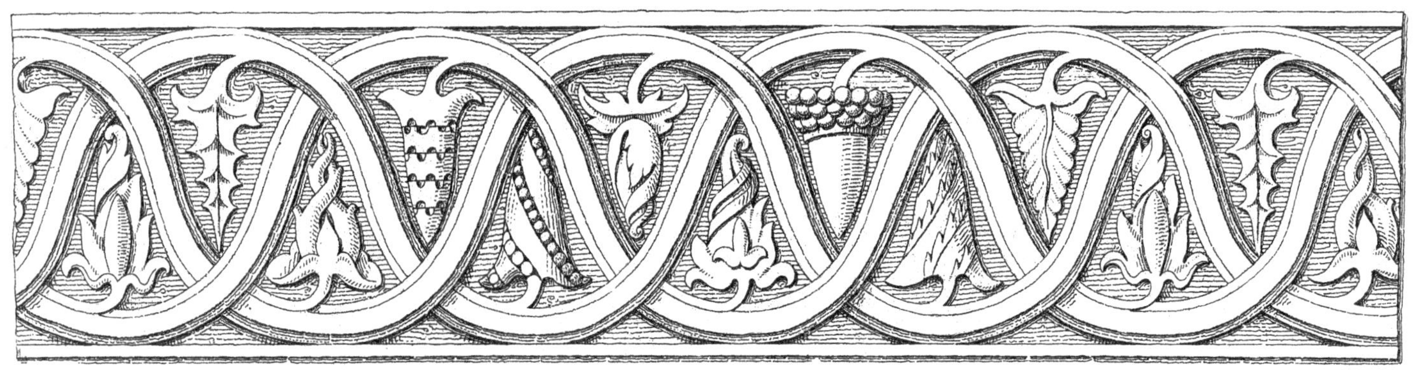

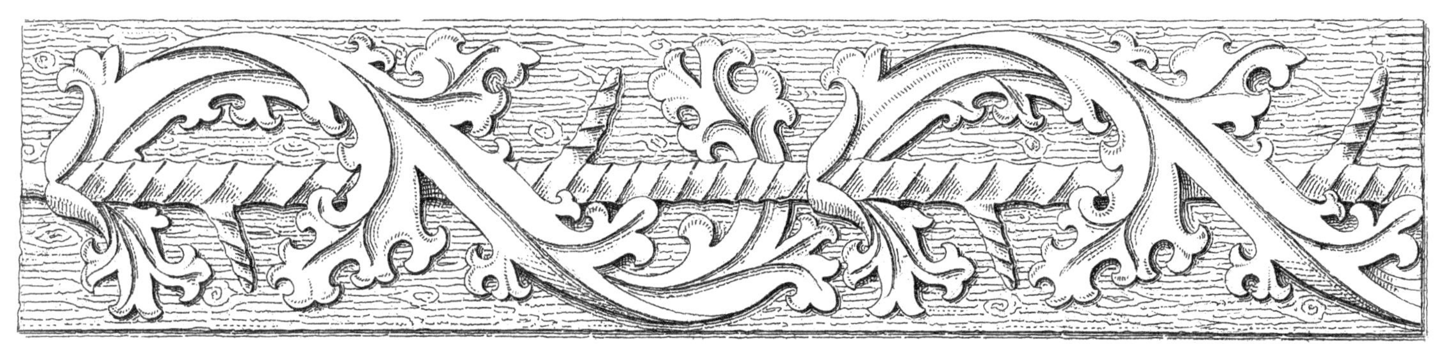

ORNAMENTS CARVED IN WOOD.

Nos 1 & 2 from Hildesheim

3 & 4 from Salzwedel.

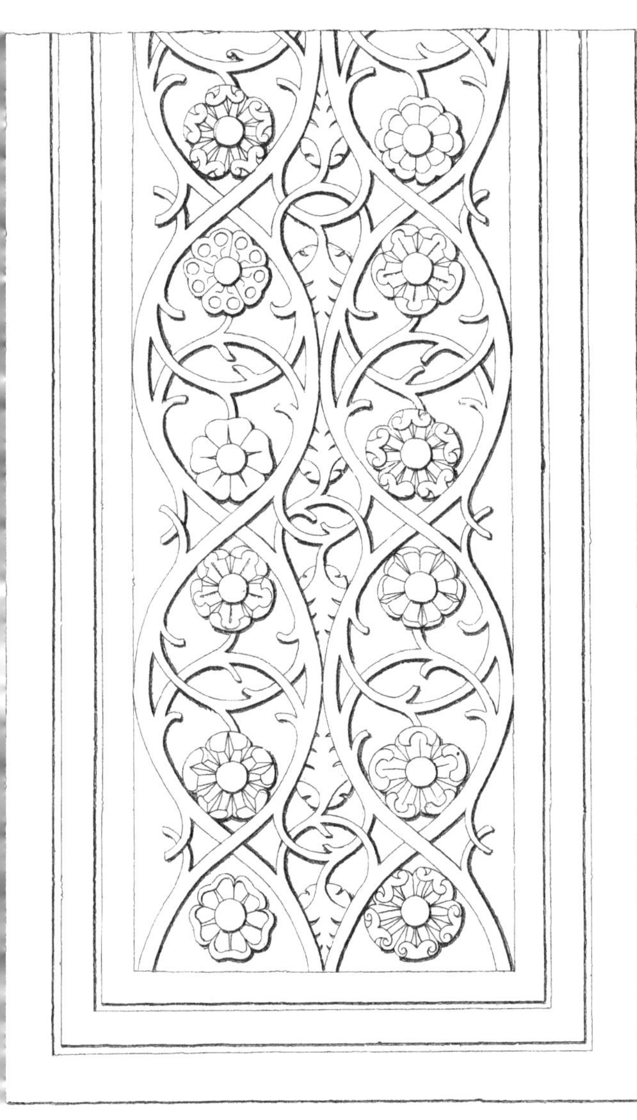

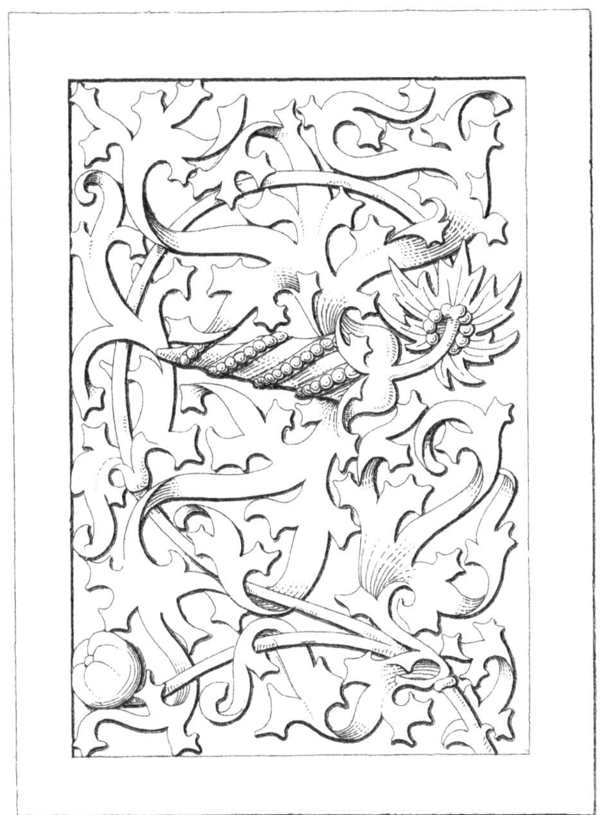

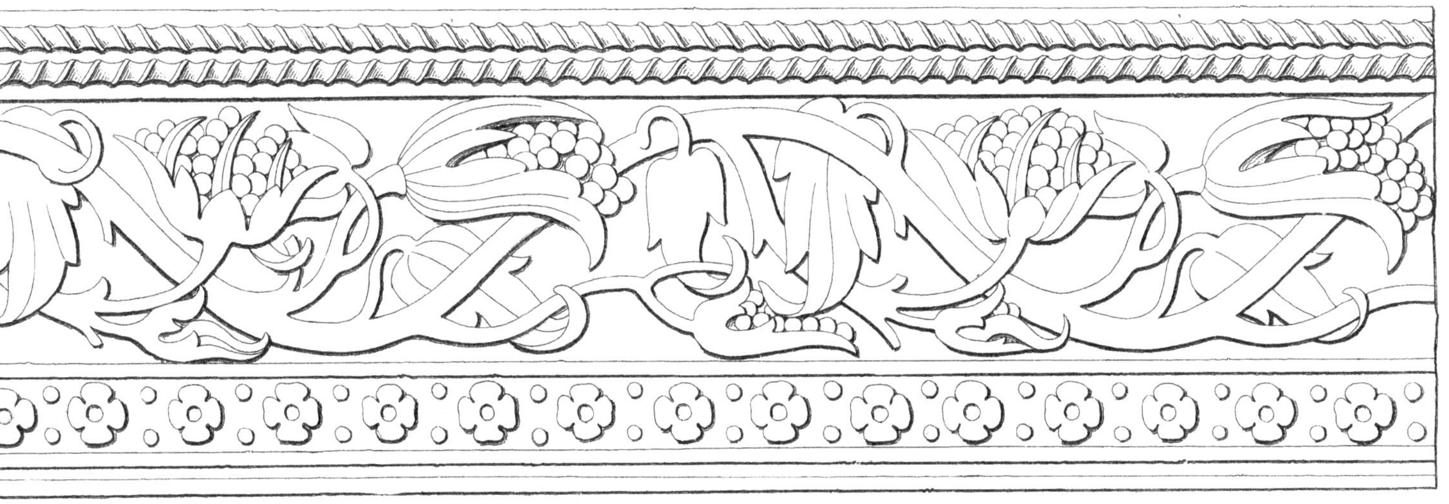

CARVINGS IN WOOD,

Date the beginning of the 16th Century.

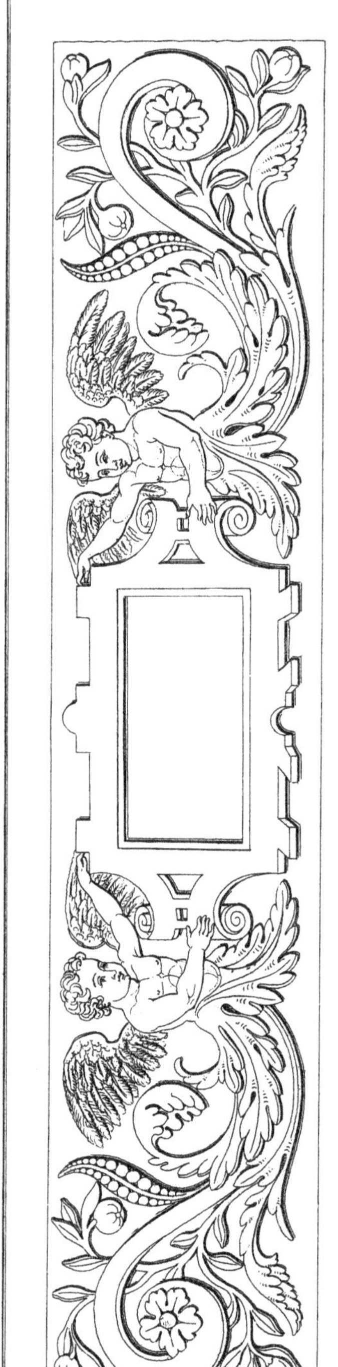

ORNAMENTS,
From the Palace of Heidelberg.
Date 1540.

1.

2.

3.

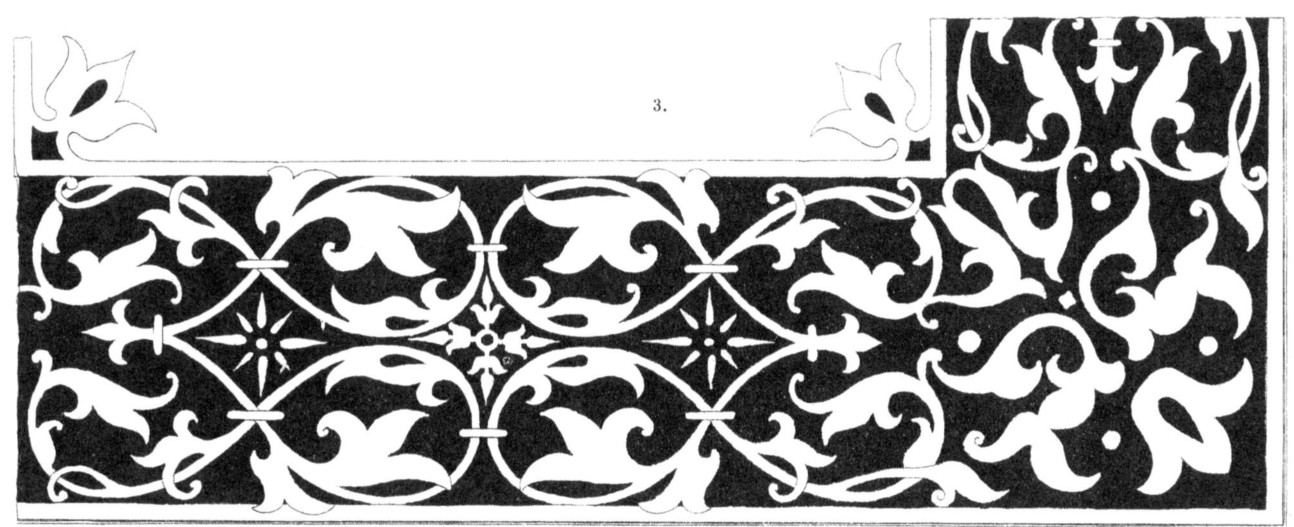

Nos. 1 & 2. From the monuments of Sophia and Maria,

Daughters of James Ist who died in 1606 & 1607.

No. 3. From the monument of the Countefs of Oxford and family.

Date 1589. All in Westminster Abbey.

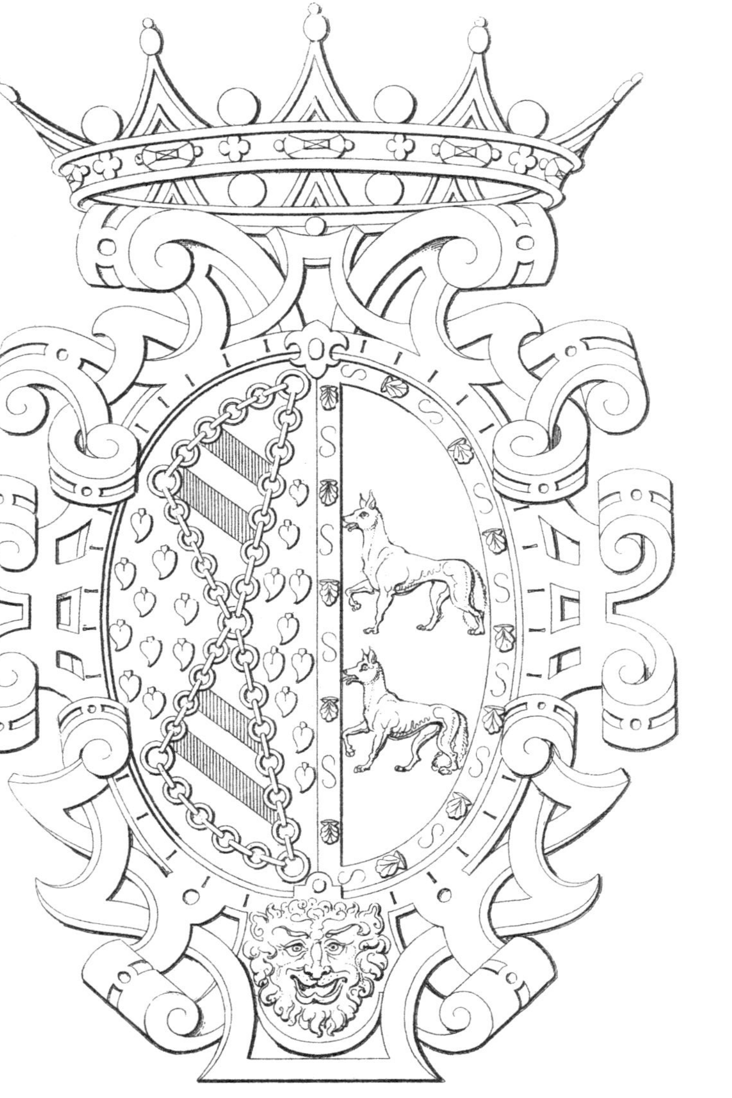

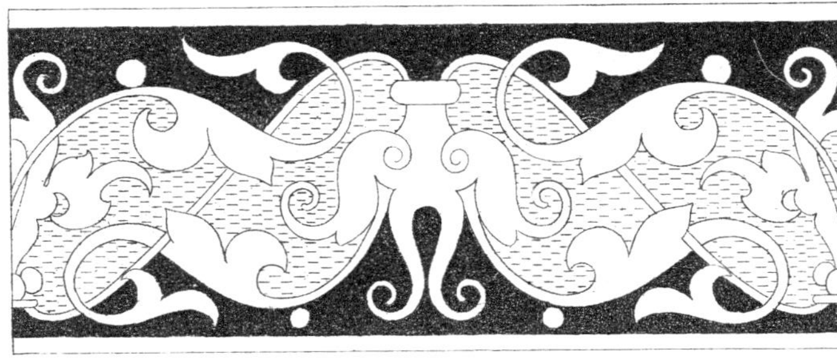

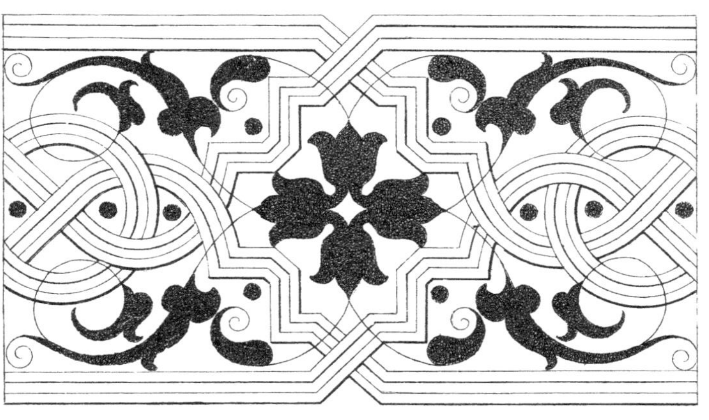

ORNAMENTS,

of the beginning of the 17th Century.

Date the end of the 15th Century.

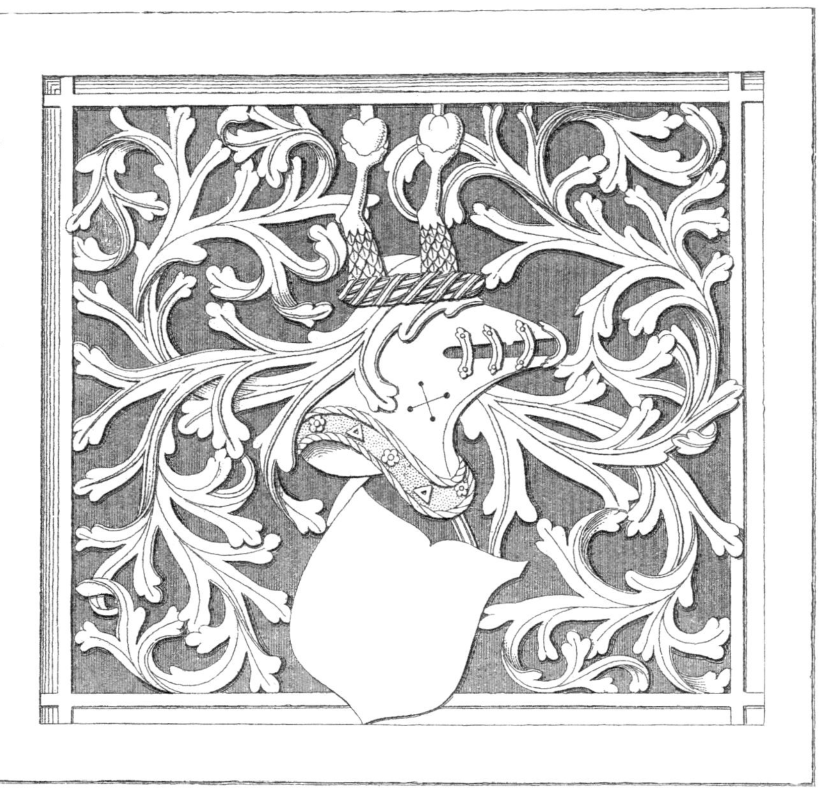

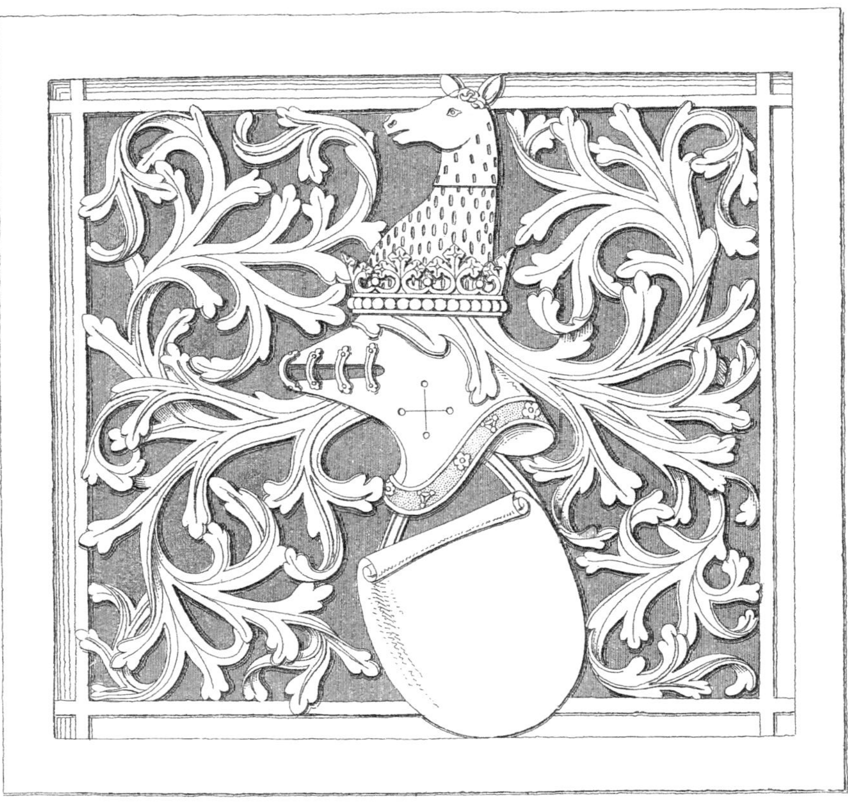

HERALDIC PANELS,

In the possession of Thos Willement, F.S.A.

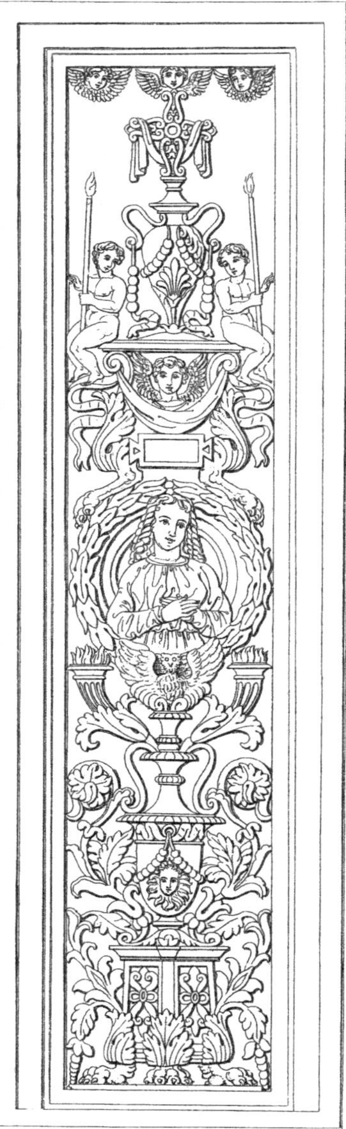

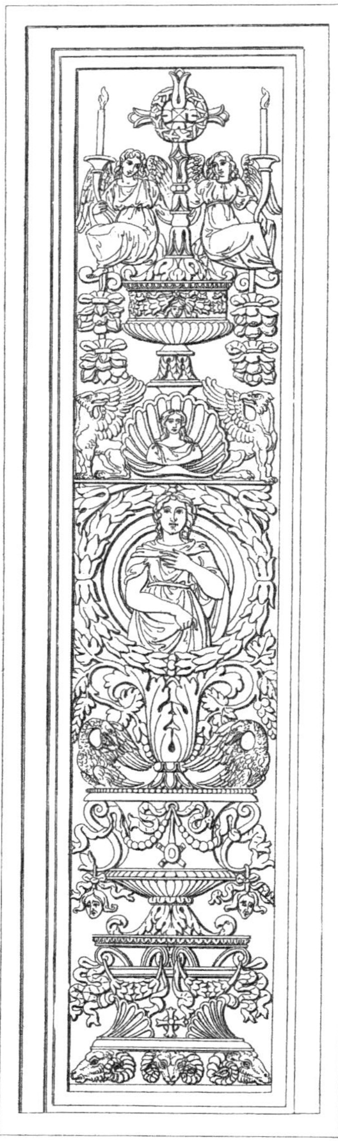

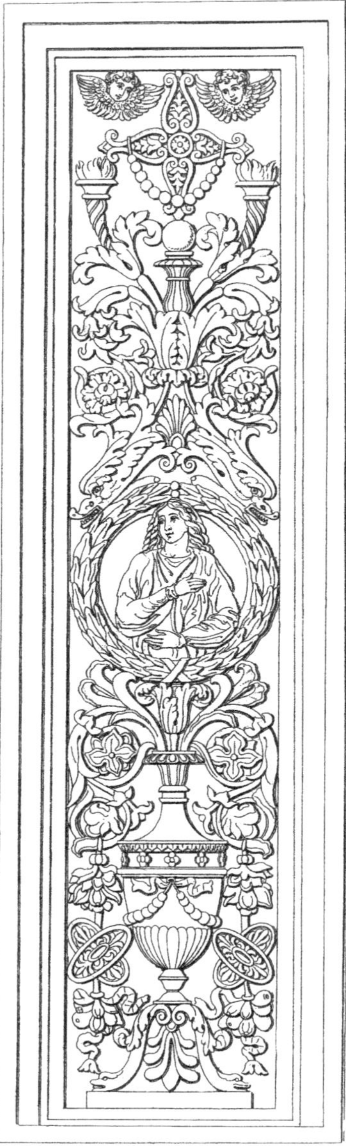

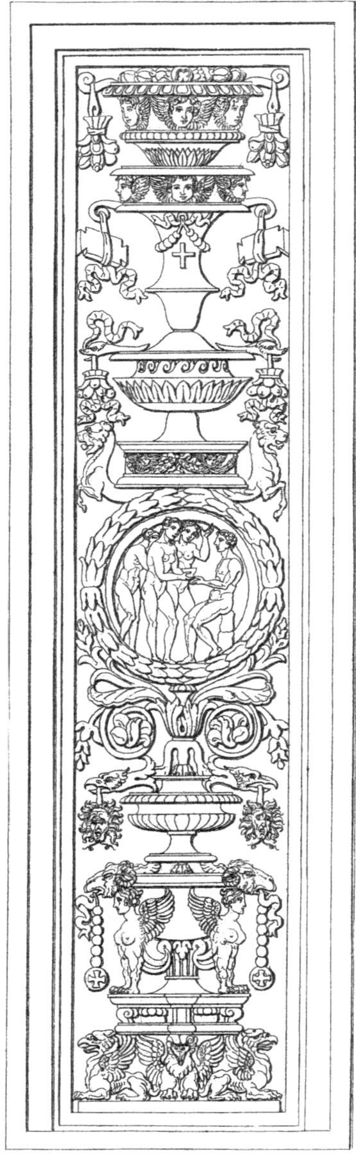

PANNELS IN MARBLE.

From the Facade of the Certosa di Pavia.

Beginning of 16th Century.

Date 1472.

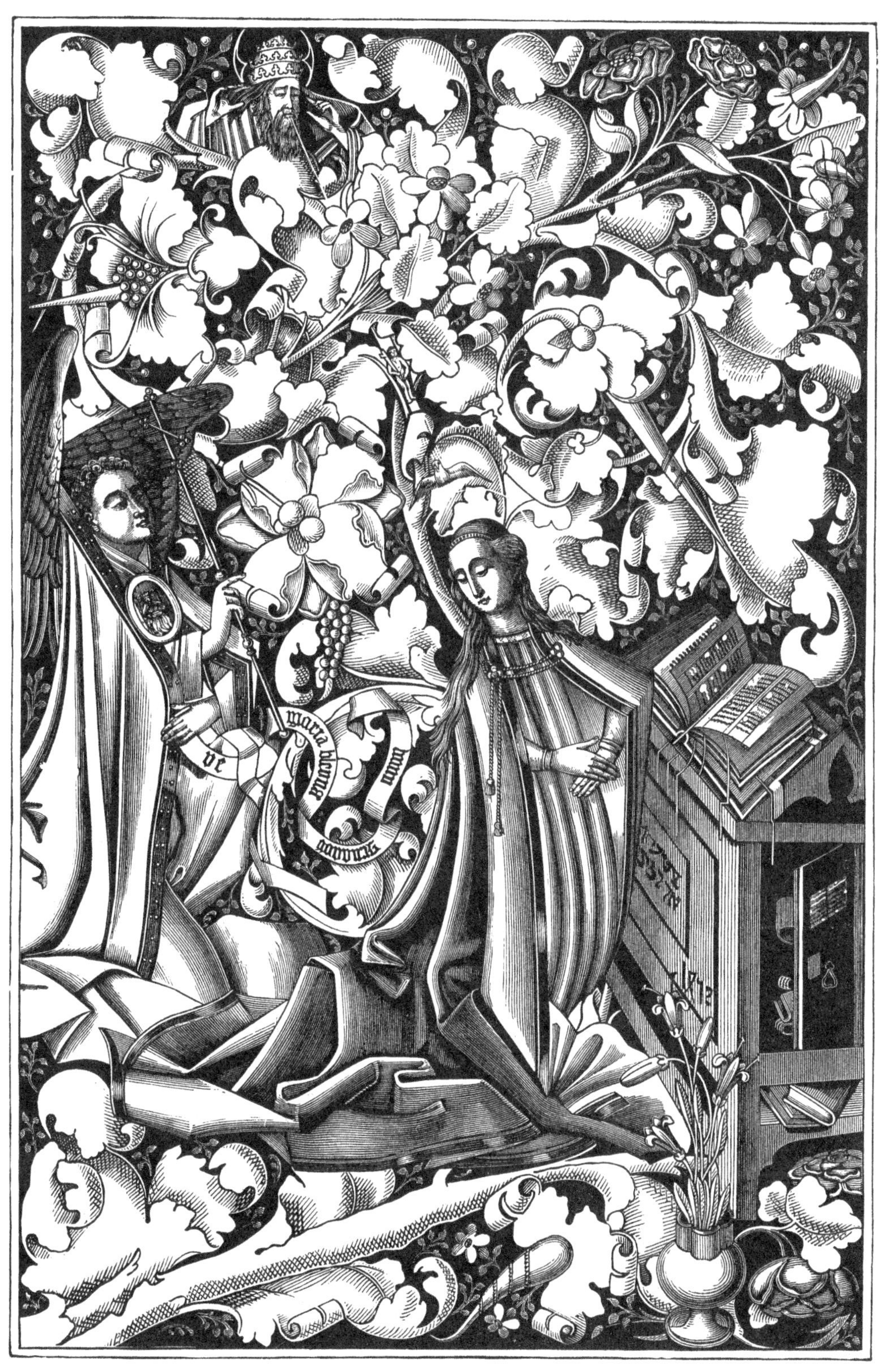

FROM AN EARLY GERMAN PICTURE.

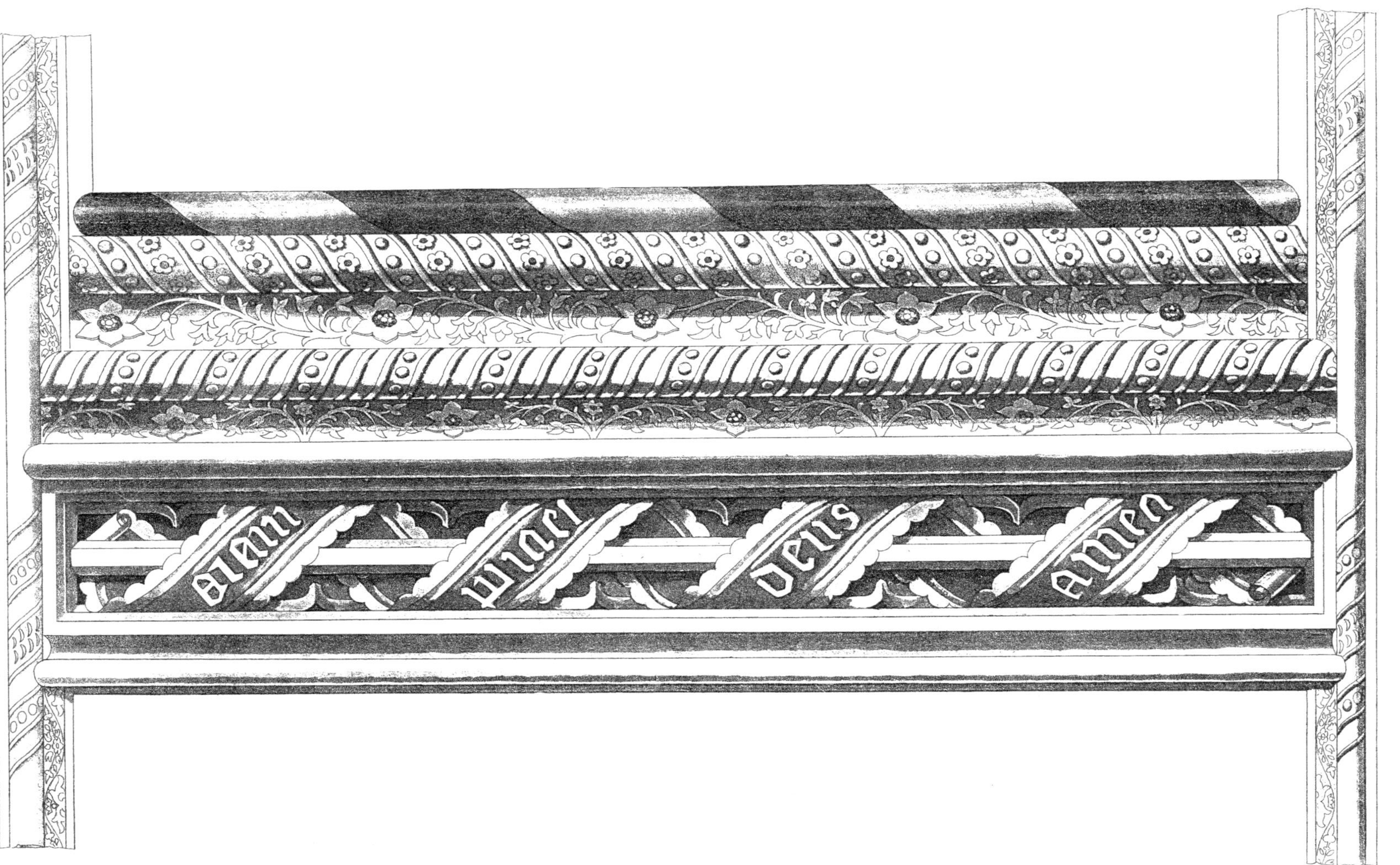

FROM A PAINTED OAK SCREEN,

In Worstead Church, Norfolk.

Date the beginning of the 16th Century.

$\frac{1}{3}$ full size.

Date the time of Edward 3rd

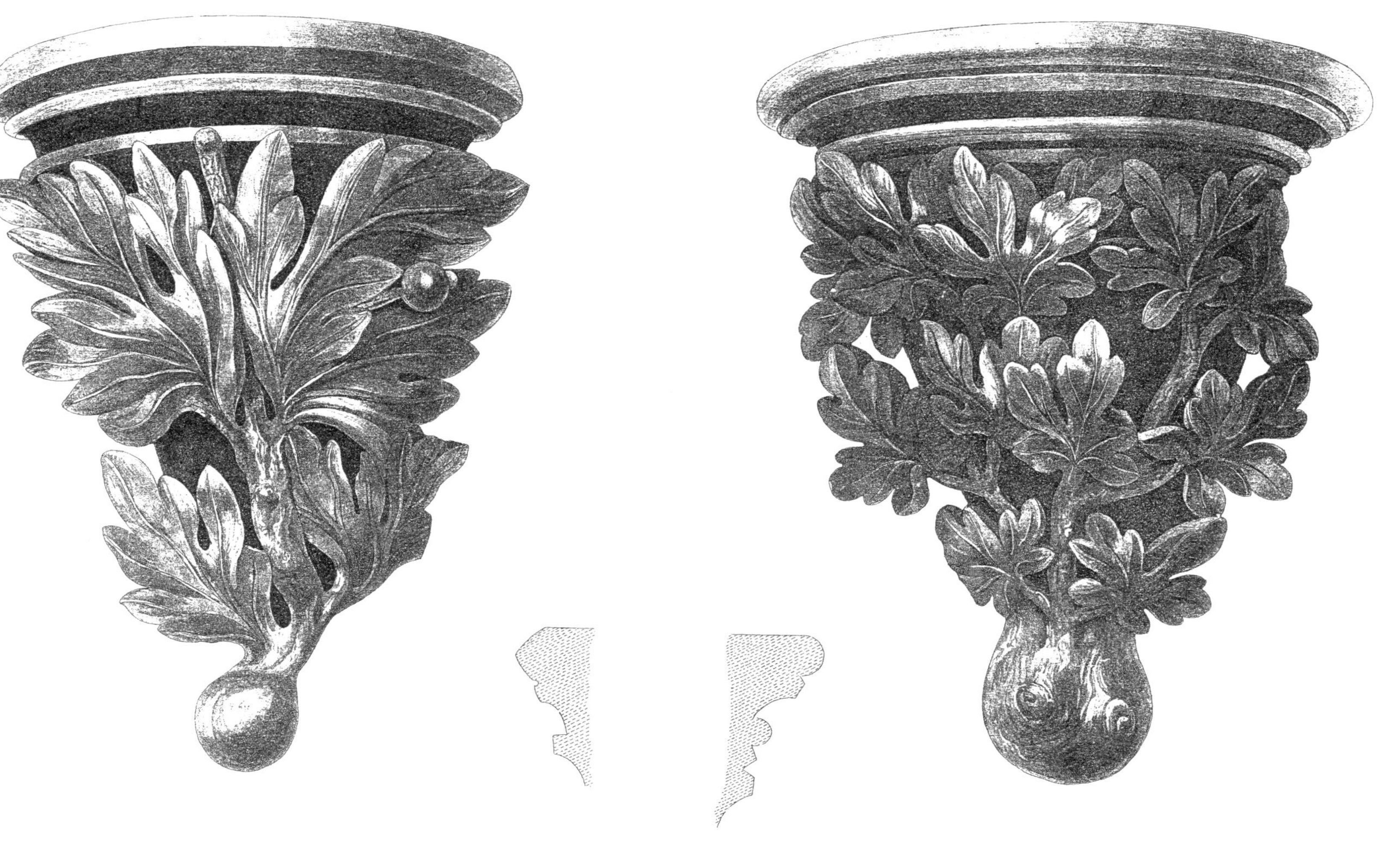

Sections of Mouldings.

P E N D A N T S,

From St. Stephen's Chapel.

¾ full size.

Capital developed. Royal Abbey of St Denys. 11th Century.

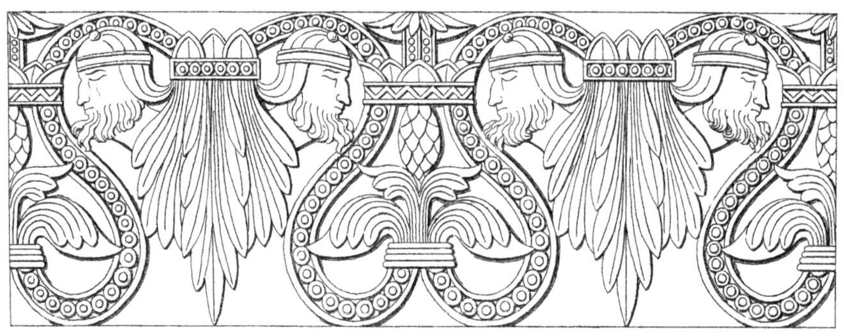

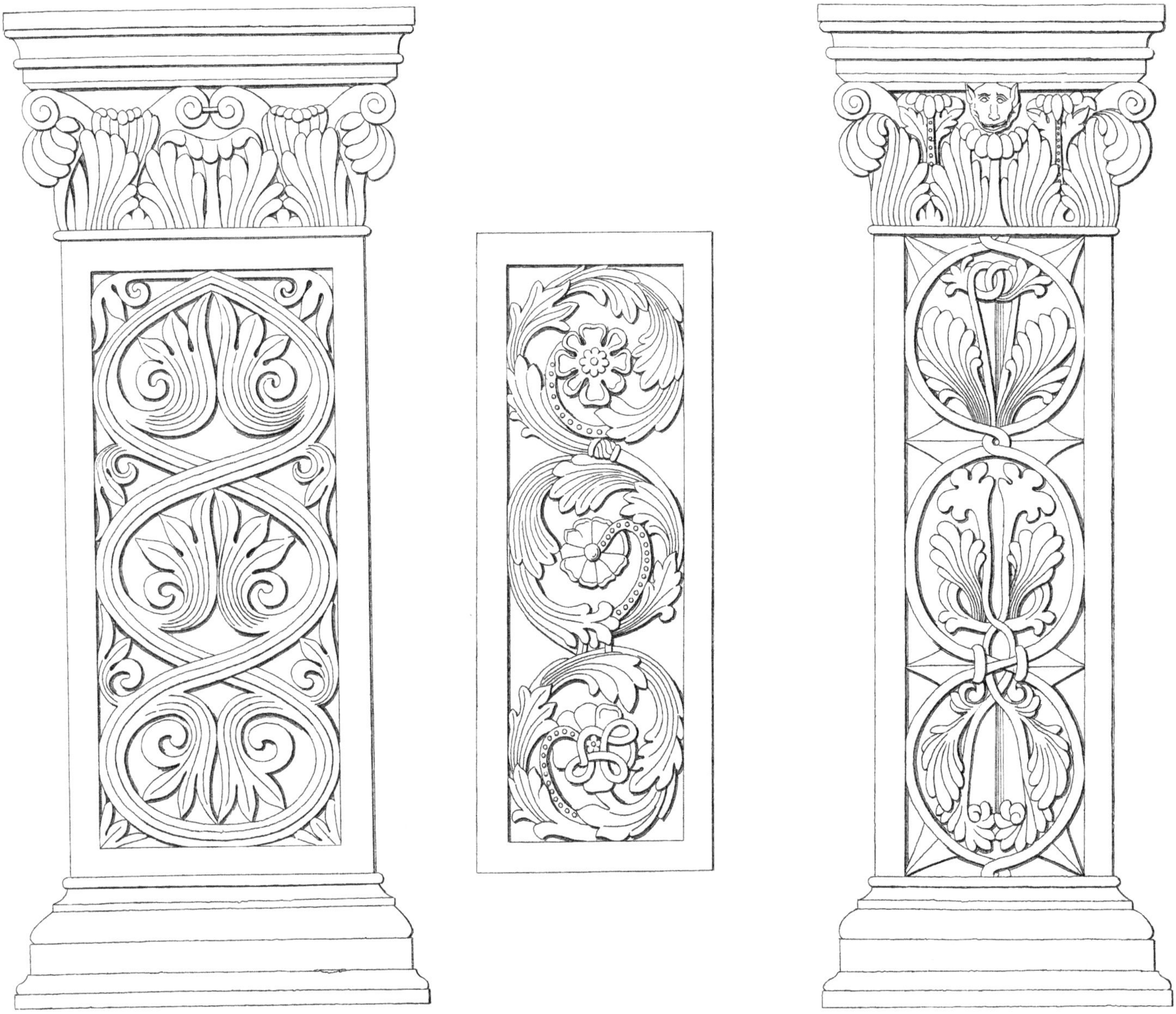

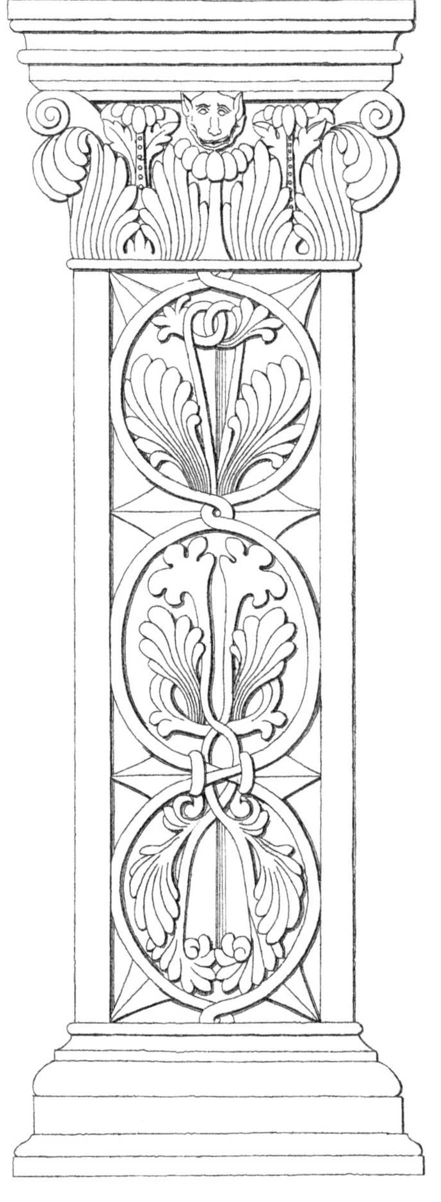

THREE SIDES OF A PILASTER,

In the Cloister of St Sauveur at Aix, in Provence.

Date the 11th Century.

Date 1637.

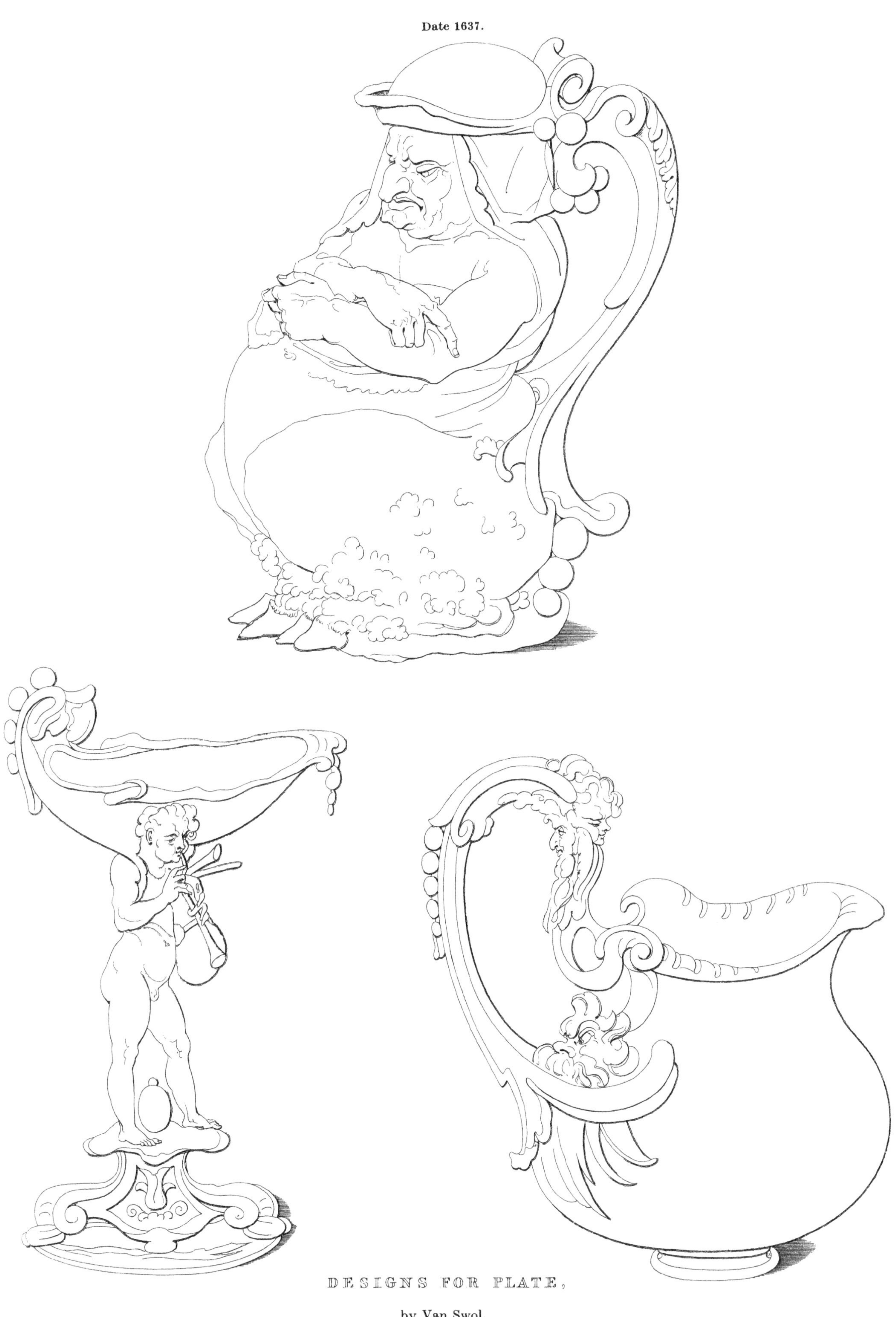

DESIGNS FOR PLATE,

by Van Swol.

BORDER OF STAINED GLASS

In the Royal Abbey

of St Denys, near Paris.

Date towards the

end of the 12th Century.

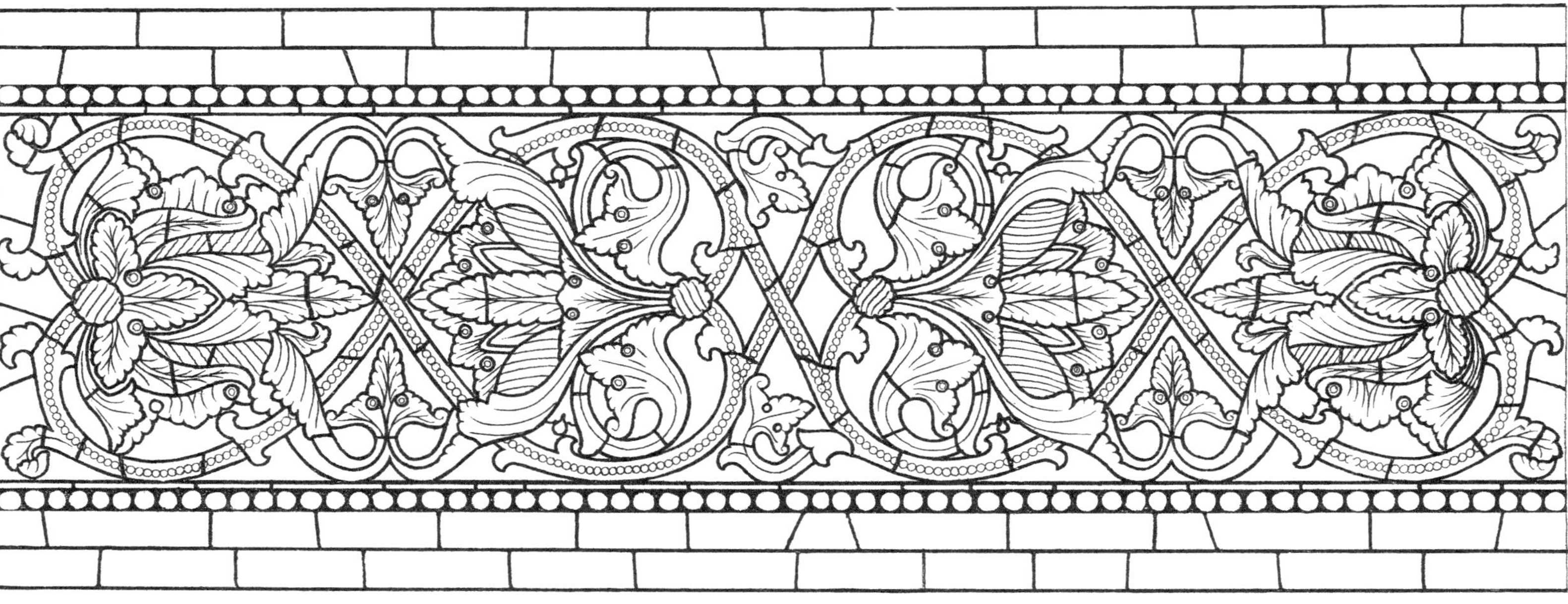

STAINED GLASS,

of the 12th Century.

In the posseſsion of T. Willement Esqr F.S.A.

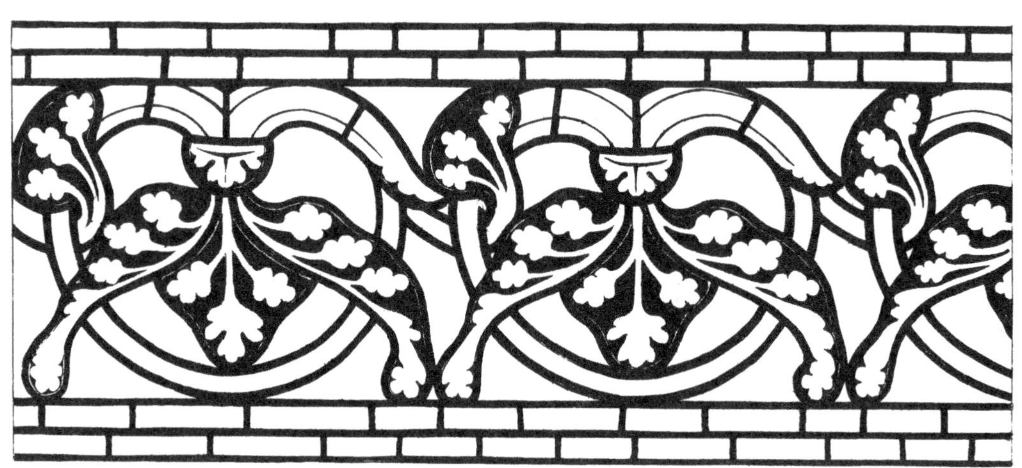

STAINED GLASS,

From Canterbury Cathedral.

Date the latter part of the 12th Century.

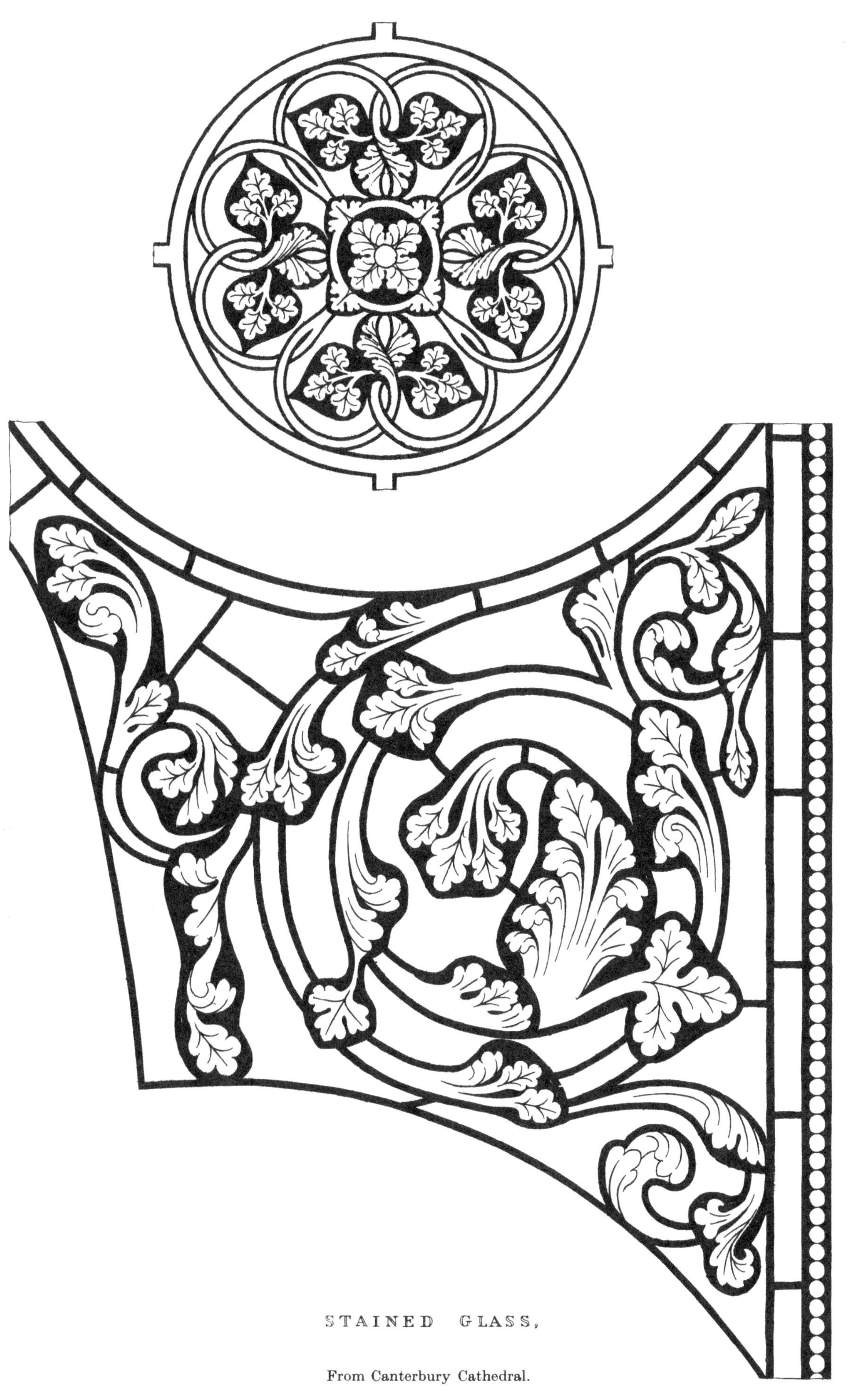

STAINED GLASS,

From Canterbury Cathedral.

Date the latter part of the 12th Century.

Date the 13th Century.

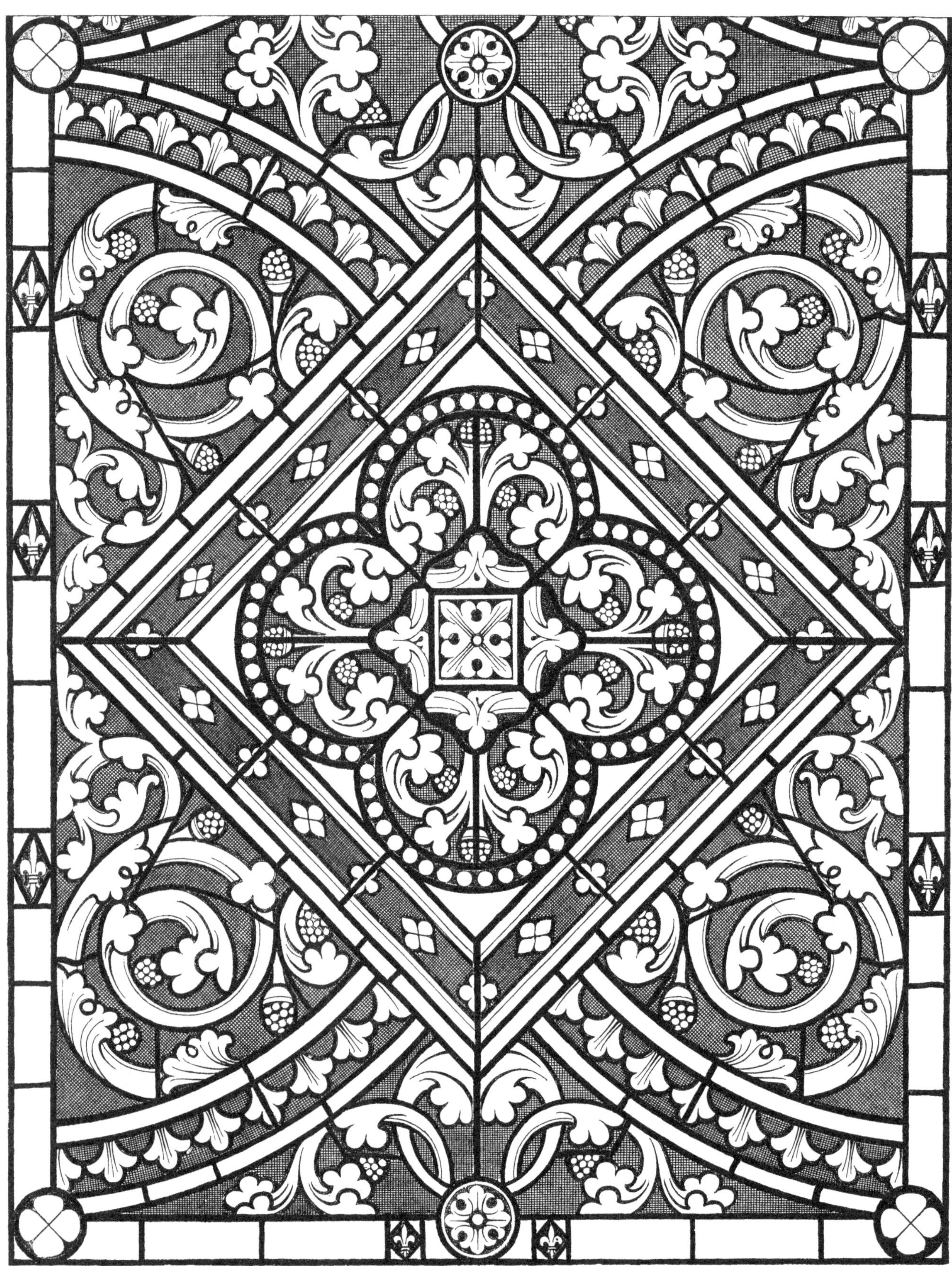

STAINED GLASS,

From Salisbury Cathedral.

Date 1307.

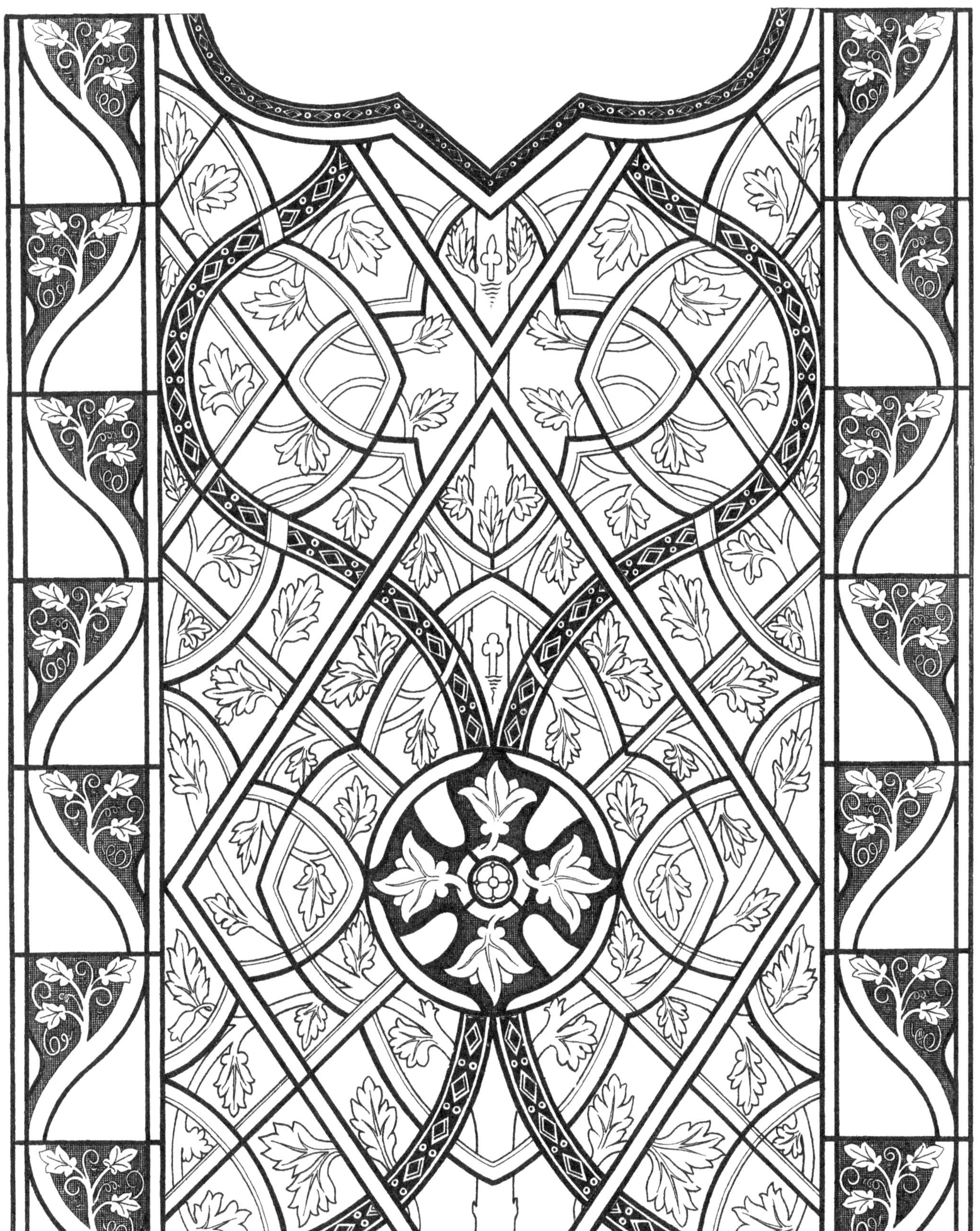

STAINED GLASS.

From the Chapter House of York Cathedral.

⅛ full size.

Date the beginning of the 14th Century.

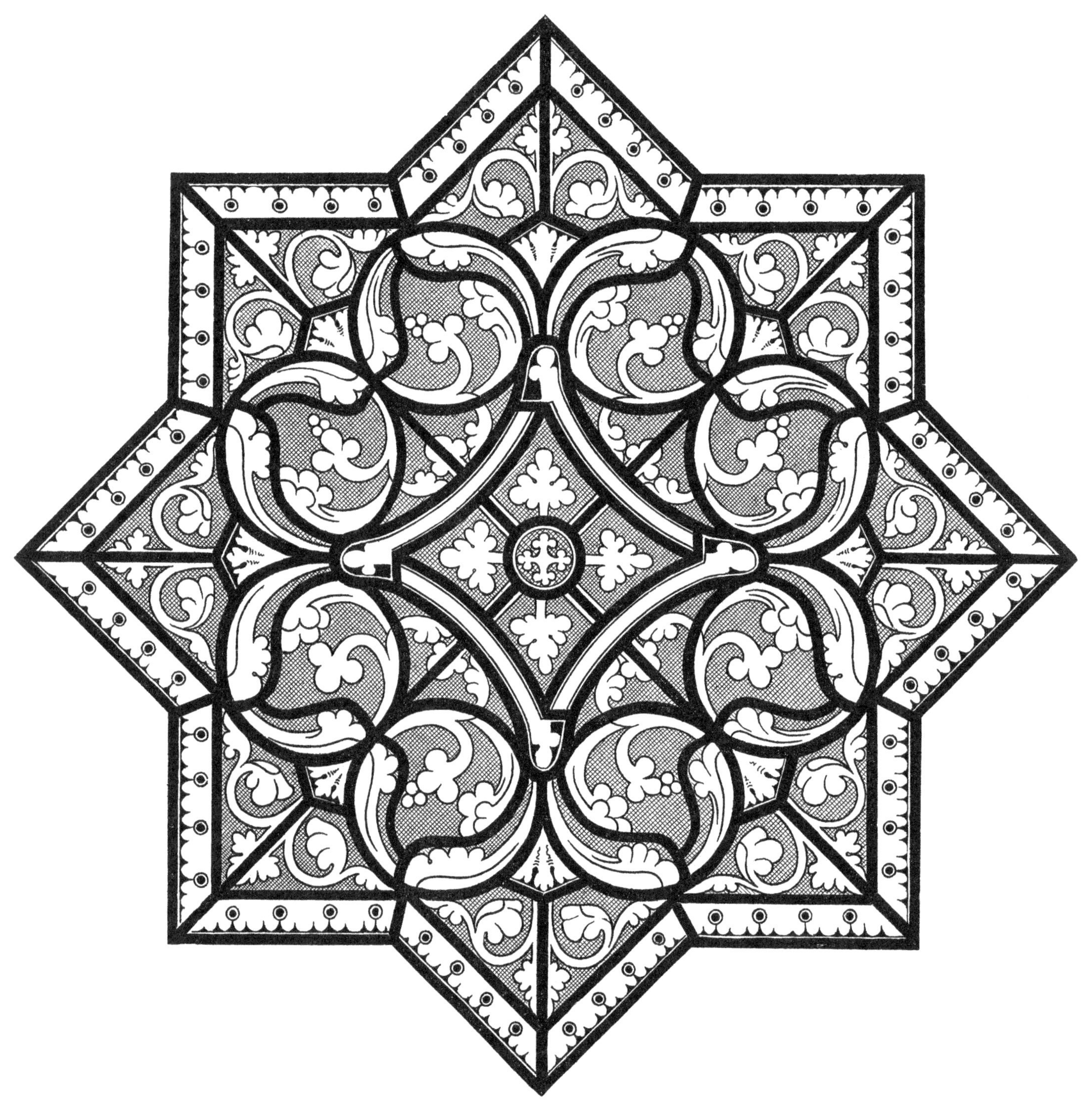

Stained Glass

From Southwell Church, Nottinghamshire.

Date, the latter part of the 14th Century.

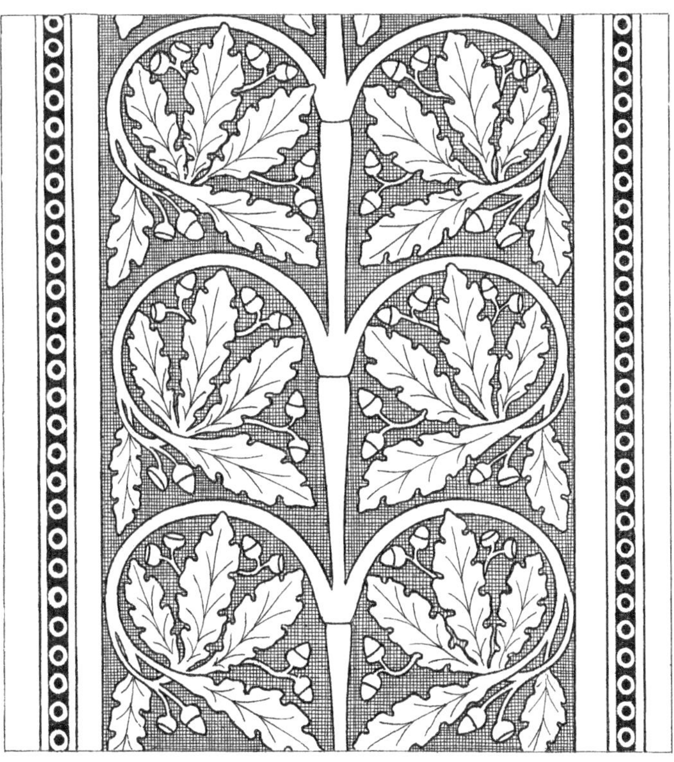

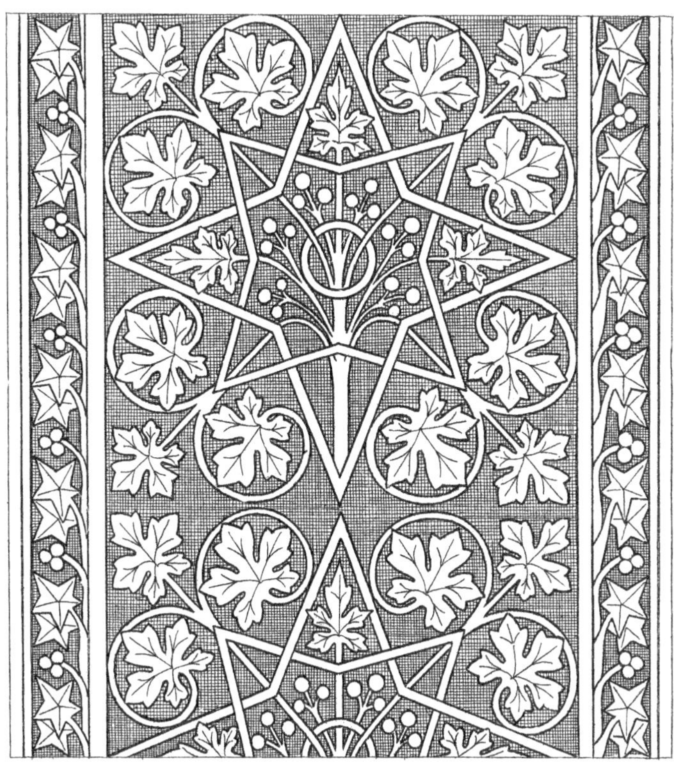

STAINED GLASS,

From the Church of Altenberg, near Cologne.

Date the 15th Century.

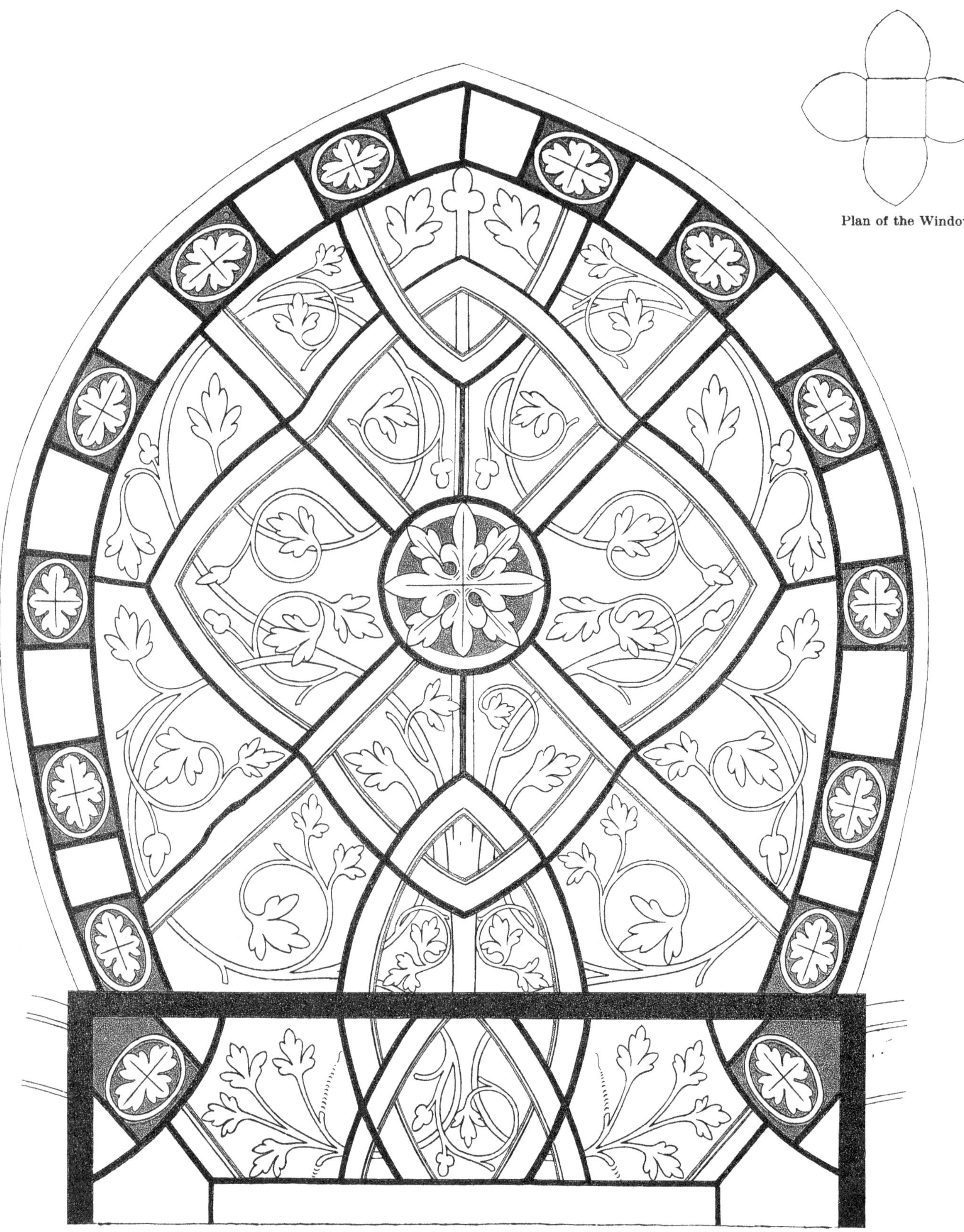

STAINED GLASS,

From the Sacristy of the Cathedral of Chartres.

H.Shaw.

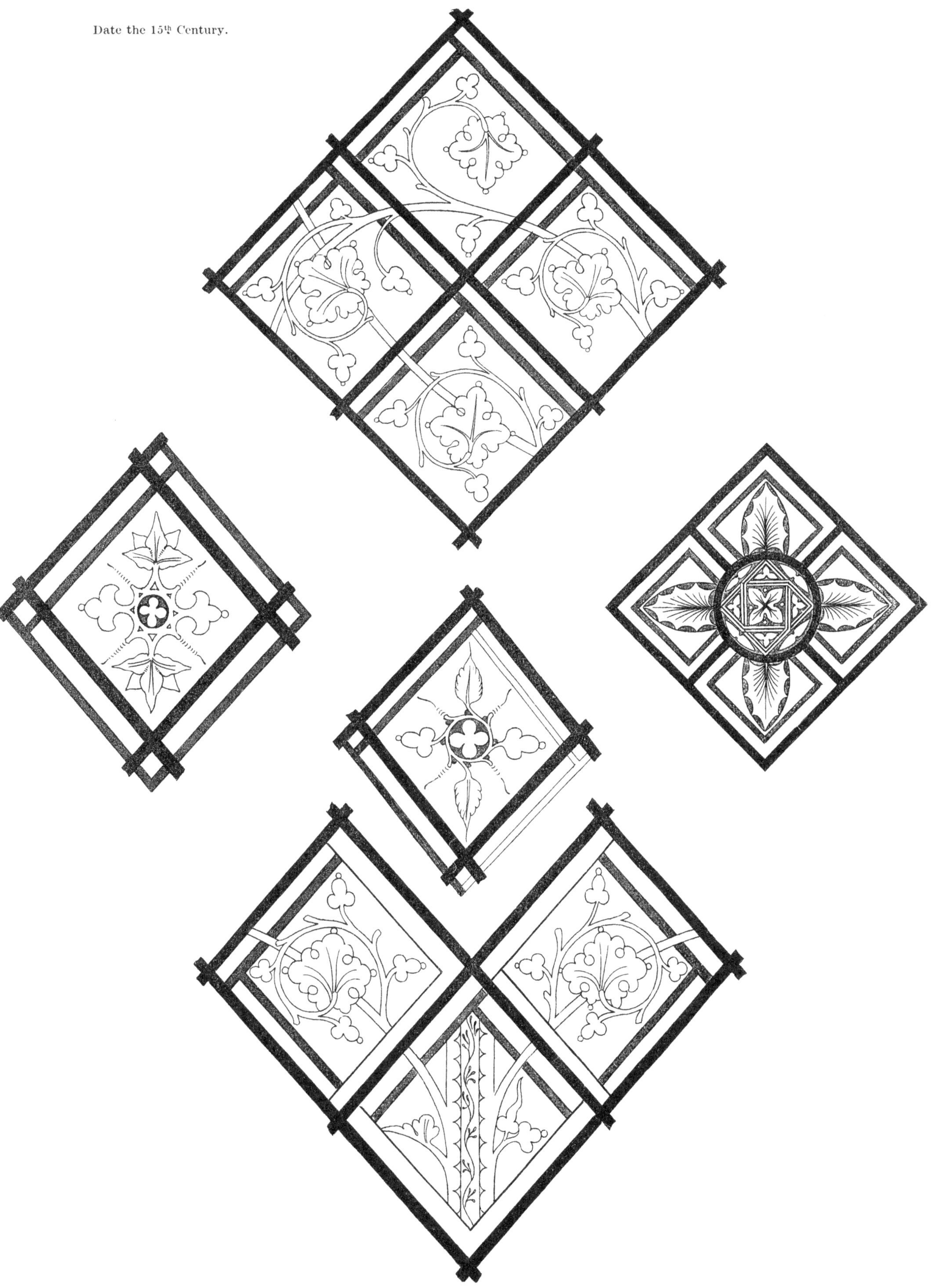

STAINED GLASS,

From the entrance to the Sacristy of the Cathedral of Chartres.

H.Shaw.

Date about the middle of 16th Century.

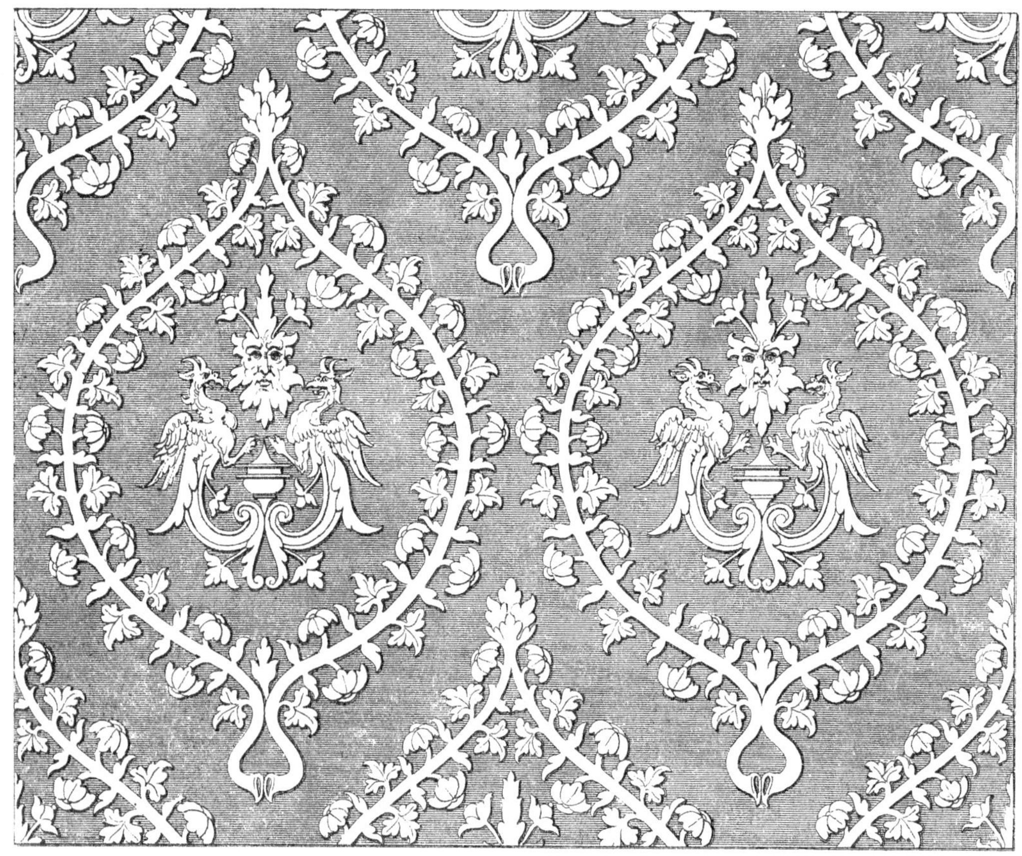

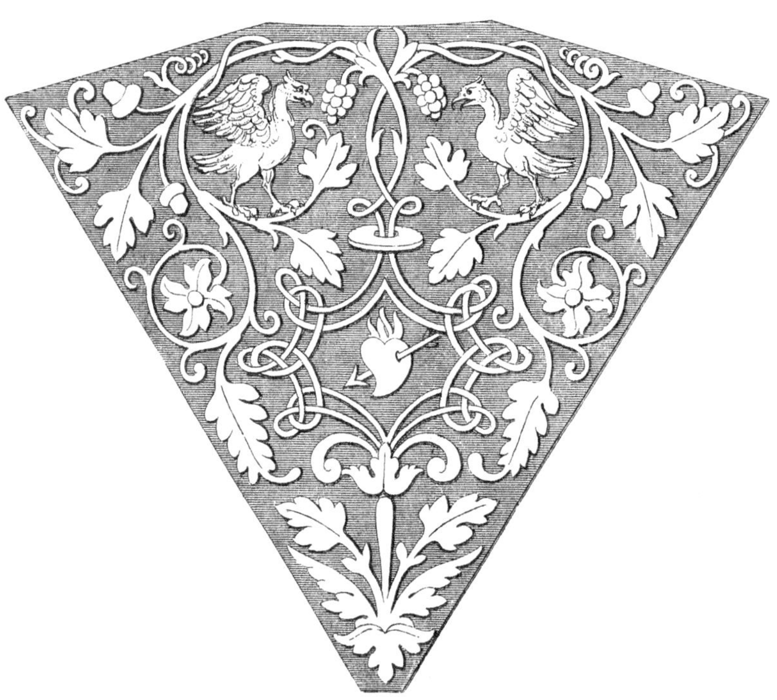

Nº 1. From stained glaſs.

Nº 2. A design for needle work.

H.Shaw.

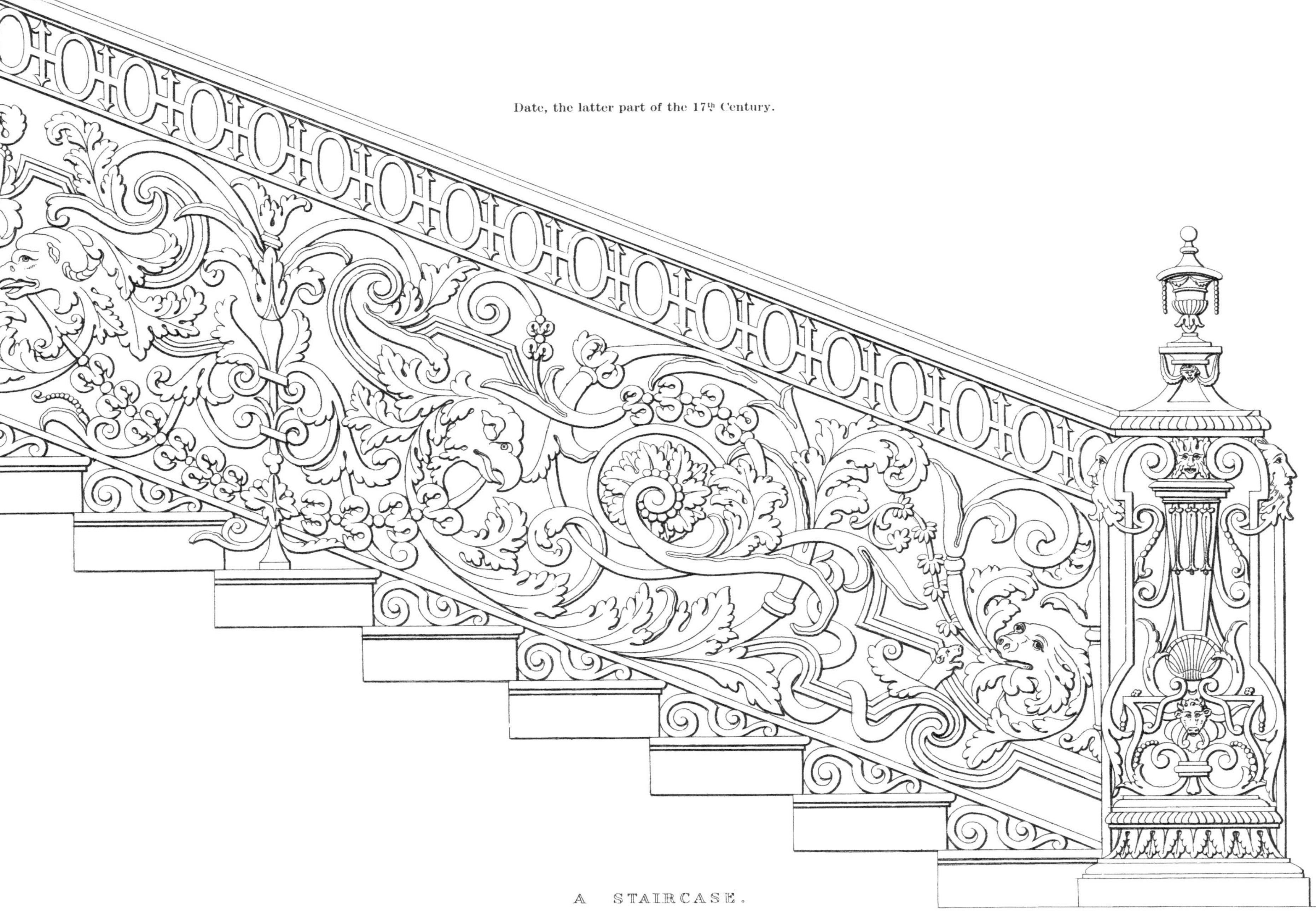

Date, the latter part of the 17th Century.

A STAIRCASE.

From a drawing in the poſseſsion of C. J. Richardson Esqr. Archt.

Date the latter part of the 17th Century.

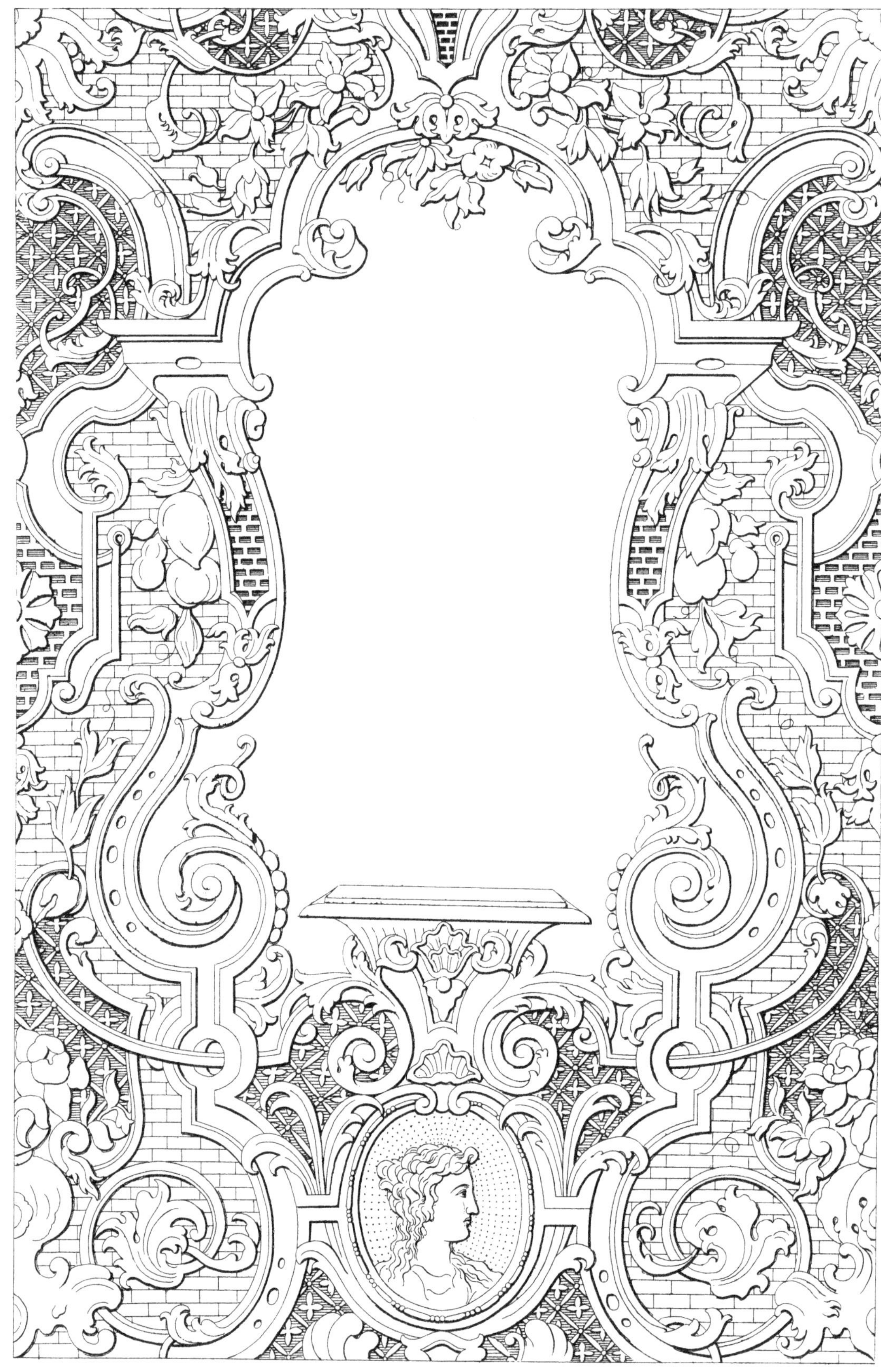

A DESIGN FOR TAPESTRY,

From a drawing in the pofsefsion of C. J. Richardson, Esq[r] Arch[t].